In Loving Memory of our son,
Brian Nicholas Hoeflinger
12/28/1994 – 2/2/2013

Life. One word that means everything to humans. Life is precious, and it is easy to forget that sometimes. B.N.H.

To Kevin, Julie, and Christie...

This time in our lives will never come again. As the focus of our family has been on Brian much of the time since his death, NEVER lose sight of how much your mother and father do truly love each of you with all our hearts. Your brother Brian has left this world unexpectedly and far too soon, but he will always remain a part of our lives forever.

The vision for this book came to me in glaring detail one night as I awoke from a dream. I quickly wrote the information down as not to forget it, since the details of a dream can quickly fade from your memory once awake. The book complete with title and chapters has remained unchanged from that night. The body of the book quickly came to me as I wrote over the course of two months through many a sleepless night. The words and emotion flowed out of me without explanation. The process then stopped as abruptly as it had started and the completed book was as I had envisioned it. As I now look back on this brief period of time, I realize that something unexplainable had overcome me in such a way that I could never reproduce the contents of this book again. That part of me is gone and has been forever imprinted in the contents of this book.

Brian F. Hoeflinger, MD

Table of Contents

Preface

The book that you are about to read is a true story and accurately represents the harsh reality of death. Like a black hole that not even light can escape, death is the final destination for everyone. It is the one constant in life that cannot be overcome or changed. Some will die sooner than others, and no explanation will be given. It is a reality that must be accepted.

This is the story of my son Brian Nicholas Hoeflinger, who died unexpectedly at age 18. His death would seem a random event in an otherwise predestined universe. The set of circumstances surrounding his death may or may not help you draw your own conclusions. As for me, as I continuously ask the question of why it had to be my son, I know there will never be an answer, but only more questions. So instead of asking why he died, I would ask you to consider why Brian Nicholas Hoeflinger lived. Was there indeed a purpose to his 18 years of life here on earth, and how has the world changed as a result of his life and his death? These are questions I have asked repeatedly through many a sleepless night.

Someday these questions will be posed to us all. I like to think that each of us has a purpose in life and time to fulfill our destiny. When our mission here is complete, we can only hope to leave this place with a feeling of peace and satisfaction as we transition from this realm to the next. Someday I would like to see my son Brian as he was when he was alive—a vibrant, happy, loving young man who brought so much happiness and joy into our lives. I need that lost part of myself back someday. But for now, I want to let people know who Brian Hoeflinger was and what lessons can be learned both from his path in life and from his untimely death.

By sharing these experiences regarding my son's death, I hope to inspire people on many different levels, not only for the betterment of themselves but for the betterment of others as well. I wish for people to understand that tragedy can and should be used to bring about positive change. It is through our own life experiences and lessons that we can make the world a better place for all to live in.

Chapter 1

The Incident

It was a Friday morning like so many in the past. I was the neurosurgeon on call for our group that particular day, February 1, 2013. I usually leave the house around 5:30 or 6:00 a.m. to get to the hospital to round on my patients and then be in the operating room or my office by 7:30, depending on the day. The house was dark and quiet, with everybody still sleeping as usual. My wife's day usually started shortly thereafter. Cindy, a forensic pathologist by training, had retired to be a full-time mom to our four kids, Brian (18), Kevin (15), Julie (14), and Christie (11).

I was lucky enough to miss the chaos of the morning with four teenagers all getting ready at the same time. Cindy typically got the kids up, made their lunches, made breakfast most mornings, and then made sure they all got to school on time—a necessary routine for the three younger ones, but not for our oldest son, Brian, who was a senior in high school. Brian had gotten himself up since the sixth grade and had always been self-sufficient. He was a typical firstborn child, mature and responsible, and yet very much a creature of habit, often eating the same thing every morning for weeks on end. He had his own routine, which worked well for him during his first three years of high school.

But in his last year, Brian had transferred from an all-boys Catholic high school to the small high school in our neighborhood. This was the school system our other three children attended, and that meant he now had to drive both Kevin and Julie to school each morning. Julie had the bad habit of running late, which then interfered with Brian's last-minute departing routine.

This particular morning was no different, and Brian needed to hurry, as they were late for school. During the drive, he was pulled over by a police officer for speeding. When asked why he was speeding, Brian explained, "We're going to be late to school because my sister made us late."

The policeman again asked, "Why were you speeding?"

Brian again replied, "Because my sister was late!"

The officer asked one more time, and by this time in the conversation, Brian must have started to get the hint that he needed to take responsibility for his actions, so he answered, "Because we were late, and I was driving too fast."

The officer gave him a break by issuing him a warning rather than a speeding ticket.

The rest of the morning was fairly routine for all of us. The kids were in school, Cindy did chores at home, and I saw patients in my office.

I took off work early that afternoon so I could be at an appointment at the pediatrician's office with our youngest, Christie, and my wife. Afterward, I drove home, while Cindy went to the pharmacy to pick up medication for Christie. On her way home, she reviewed all of the kids' plans in her head for that night, including who needed a ride where and when.

She called Brian to see if he could drop Kevin off at his JV basketball game, and Brian told her that he already had plans to go out to eat with a couple of friends. He also mentioned that Texas snowmobiler Caleb Moore had died. Cindy and Brian had watched Moore crash at the Winter X Games on TV the week before while they were in Chapel Hill, North Carolina, for a college tour of the University of North Carolina, his first choice in colleges. Brian said it was the first time in his life that someone had died after he witnessed their injury on TV. This event seemed to shake him up and touch him in an odd way.

Then he told his mom about the warning he had received that morning for speeding. Cindy reminded him about his fender bender in the Barnes & Noble parking lot the previous week. "You really need to be more careful," she chastised him.

"I know, Mom. I'm not stupid."

"You know bad things happen in threes."

He smirked and replied, "Okay, Mom. You are so weird. I'm not superstitious."

"No, Brian, I really believe that. It's happened to me before."

"Yeah right, Mom."

It was just after their phone call that I arrived home around 4:30 that afternoon. Brian was standing next to the refrigerator in the kitchen when I asked him if he wanted to go work out with me. We had started to work out together several times a week at a local gym. He told me that he was going out with friends to grab a bite to eat, so he couldn't.

That was the last time I ever spoke to Brian. As it turns out, he and two of his friends drove to a state liquor store, walked in together, and bought a 1.75-liter bottle of Belvedere vodka. Three young-looking teenagers bought vodka without being carded. Afterward, they went to

Jimmy John's to grab a bite to eat, but apparently Brian did not eat. When he was dropped off back home with his friend Michael, Christie ran up to them, yelling, "Brian, my favorite brother!" and gave him a big hug.

"Why do you only hug me when my friends are around?" he asked with a grin.

We all went to the basketball game that night, but separately. Kevin arrived early to play in the JV game. Cindy, Christie, and I went to watch Kevin's game, while Julie and her friend Phoebe stayed behind to finish their outfits. The theme of the night was "hurt night," so the kids attended the game on crutches, with bandages around their heads, and in doctors' scrubs and white coats. Michael and Brian were hanging out in the basement and planned to come a little later.

The boys' varsity basketball team easily defeated their opponents, winning 51-33, and by that time our whole family was there to watch. The student body cheering section yelled and screamed, especially enjoying the fact that BCSN, our local sports station, was there to record the entire game. Cindy and I saw Brian cheering with his friends and having fun. That was the last time we ever saw Brian alive.

The game ran late that evening. We were all going to go out for dinner, but because it was late and I was on call, I wanted to get home to get some sleep in case I was called into the hospital for an emergency. While Christie came home with me, Cindy dropped Kevin off at a friend's house for a sleepover and took Julie and her friend out to dinner at an Italian restaurant near our house. Julie was particularly animated that night, my wife tells me, even getting up at one point to sing and dance to a medley of Michael Jackson hits.

Brian had driven his car to the game. Apparently he was supposed to be picked up by a friend that night, but through a series of unfortunate events, he ended up driving his car. After the game ended, around 9:30, Brian and his friends went to a birthday party. The party was in the basement of a friend's house and unsupervised. The kids all brought their own drinks, meaning alcohol, including the 1.75-liter bottle of Belvedere vodka that Brian and his friends had bought earlier.

From what we've learned, Brian was texting throughout the evening and acting like himself, other than having drinks of vodka. Around 11:30, as the party was breaking up, an argument of sorts started. Brian tried to leave, and someone tried to stop him by taking his car keys away. Brian lay down on the floor, pretending to sleep. Another boy was in the bathroom vomiting, with several friends attending to him. During this brief hiatus of confusion, Brian leaped up, grabbed his keys, and ran up the stairs and out of the house. He jumped in his car and locked the doors.

A friend of Brian's who was apparently the "designated" driver that evening followed Brian outside and stood in front of the car while Brian started it and revved the engine. The friend stood there briefly, trying to stop Brian from leaving, but Brian was persistent. The boy soon gave up, and Brian drove off around 11:45.

Soon thereafter, at approximately 11:50, Brian's car struck a tree in our neighborhood at high speed.

A patrolling police officer was driving by at about that time. He saw a fire in the woods and called it in. As he approached the crash site, he saw Brian's demolished car on fire.

We spoke to him at Brian's funeral, and he described the sequence of events as he choked back tears. When he arrived, Brian was unconscious but with a faint heartbeat and barely breathing. His seat belt was on. The officer grabbed a fire extinguisher to keep the fire in the engine compartment at bay until help arrived. As responding units arrived, the officers and paramedics tried to free Brian's trapped body from the wreckage, but his lower body was stuck because the dashboard and firewall had been pushed into the driver's seat. Turns were taken with alternating fire extinguishers to keep the increasing fire down. With tears in his eyes and his voice shaking, the officer recalled thinking to himself that he was not going to let this young man die in that car, engulfed in fire.

Finally, five of the responders all pulled at once and freed Brian's body from the car. As they were moving him to the ambulance nearby, the car exploded and was engulfed in flames. No one else was hurt that night.

Cindy and I were sleeping when our doorbell rang at 1:00 a.m. I sprang out of bed, and when I opened the door, I was confronted with three of Brian's friends frantically looking for him and wondering if we had seen him. I told them we had not seen Brian since the basketball game.

Cindy came downstairs and asked what was going on. The boys said that they had been at a party hanging out together earlier in the evening and Brian had left angry. They indicated that they had been looking for him for well over an hour and could not find him.

This didn't make sense. Brian never just "disappeared," and it would have been very out of character for him to be angry. We both immediately began calling and texting him, but got no response. This was also out of character for Brian, because he always answered calls and texts. My wife had just texted him at 10:30 that night to remind him that he needed to pick up his date's corsage tomorrow for the turnabout dance and that senior pictures were tomorrow as well. He promptly texted her back as he always did and said he would pick up the corsage and be there for senior pictures.

On one level, we both knew that something was horribly wrong. On the other hand, we still hoped that if we could just figure out where Brian was, everything would be okay. Should we call other parents—in the middle of the night?

As Cindy paced the halls, our phone rang. It was the mother of one of Brian's friends. She said Brian had been in an accident. I'll never forget my wife's response that night as long as I live—the sheer horror and emotion in her voice when she responded, "Oh God, no! Please, no! Not Brian!"

My heart began to race. The woman told us that Brian had been taken to St. Anne's hospital, a level-three trauma center for minor injuries only. I was the on-call surgeon for neurosurgery trauma that weekend for both St. Anne's and Toledo Hospital, a level-one trauma center for major life-threatening injuries. I frantically called St. Anne's ER, my hands trembling, and asked them if my son had been brought there.

There was an uncomfortable pause, followed by the response, "You need to go to Toledo Hospital right now."

I reiterated, "This is Dr. Hoeflinger, and I want to know what is happening with my son!"

"We can't tell you anything. You need to go straight to Toledo

Hospital."

At that moment, my whole life changed. I knew Brian must have been in a terrible accident and was severely injured.

I started to hyperventilate, and my body began to tremble uncontrollably. I could barely hold the phone as I called Toledo Hospital's ER to ask if my son had been brought there. Again there was a deafening pause, after which I was told, "Dr. Hoeflinger, you need to come to the hospital right now." No details would be given to me.

"This is Dr. Hoeflinger," I repeated, "and I need to know if my son is there and what has happened to him!" I asked to speak to the attending trauma physician on call, Dr. Dziad, whom Cindy and I knew very well.

Again in a somber and flat tone I was told, "You need to come to the ER now."

When no one would speak to me about my son, I knew that Brian was dead. What a sickening feeling to know that something horrible and permanent had happened to my child and there was nothing I could do to change it.

Cindy called a friend to come and stay with the girls while we drove to the hospital. I vividly remember the ride in my Jeep Grand Cherokee. The weather was cold, and it began to snow. I told Cindy that no one at the hospitals would tell me what had happened to Brian, which meant that he was seriously injured or, more likely, dead. Our bodies were numb in disbelief.

Then we both had the most hideous, yet compassionate thought a parent can have about his or her own child: we prayed that Brian was dead and not badly maimed, to be left a mere vegetable. What a horrible thing for a parent to wish for. But at that moment, it seemed like the most humane thing to wish for. The hardest emotion to describe in words is the realization that Brian had been severely injured, and our wonderful life with the boy we had seen just hours ago was gone forever.

When we arrived at the back entrance of the ER, we were met by Dr. Dziad. It was surreal to straddle both worlds that night, both of us being medical doctors but, more importantly, scared parents. I quickly asked Dr. Dziad what was happening with Brian. He told us in a somber, yet gentle tone, "Brian is dead."

We stood there for a moment in disbelief, not knowing what to feel or do. Then we walked slowly through the sliding doors. I heard Cindy murmuring, "Not my Brian. It can't be Brian. He's such a good boy. It can't be." Dr. Dziad hugged her as she started to cry.

My body and mind were painfully numb. There are no words to describe precisely what we were feeling. Our beautiful, smart, happy boy, who had brought so much love and happiness into our lives for 18 years, was dead.

We slowly walked down the back hall of the emergency department and made our way to trauma room 24. There we found our son lying motionless on a cold gurney with a white sheet covering his body up to his neck. His face was pale and cool to the touch. He looked as though he could be sleeping, and I wished he was just sleeping but knew all too well that he was dead and never to return home with us again. The finality of the moment was excruciating, as it is the finality that forces you to realize that your life can never be the same or go back to the way it was before. That exact feeling, or emotion as you may call it, is indescribable.

The next thing I remember is standing next to Brian's dead body and softly petting his hair, as I had done so many times when he was a little boy when I put him to bed. It was as if I were trying to comfort him one last time, to let him know everything would be okay. His eyelids would not stay closed, even though I tried over and over to close them. There was nothing I could do to fix this, just like there was nothing I could do to keep him from lying there dead. His face looked beautiful, with no scratches, cuts, or burns. He looked just the way he had always looked. I did not pull the sheets back, because I wanted to remember my son the way I always envisioned him and not the way the car accident had left him.

Cindy touched his forehead and ran her hand across his hair, which he had gelled up. He had been letting it grow. She walked to his left side and pulled back the sheet to touch his bare arm. "He's cold," she said.

"That's because he's dead, Cindy."

Two doctors having a conversation, but not really. She knew why he was cold, and I knew she knew, but her brain, like mine, couldn't process it.

As we walked out of the room, a state trooper stopped us to give his condolences and explained to us that Brian's car had struck a tree at high speed. The cause was unknown. He was wearing his seat belt, and the air bags had deployed. The officer asked if we knew where Brian's cell phone was, and we told him we had no idea. We thought he might know, as he was at the scene of the accident.

"Could Brian have been drinking?" he asked.

We couldn't imagine Brian drinking. No one had said anything about alcohol.

"Brian does not—did not—drink," I said, and we walked away.

Cindy and I now needed to make the decision whether to bring our kids to the hospital to see their big brother one last time. We had called friends to stay with the girls while we went to the hospital. We had Kevin brought home from a friend's house where he had been spending the night.

When we arrived back home, I gathered the kids in the kitchen. I felt inhumane for the pain I was about to inflict upon them. I will never forget their reactions as I told them that Brian was dead. Christie started to scream uncontrollably that we were lying to her and it wasn't true. Julie was initially quiet, but then started to cry, the tears for a brother she would never have again gently falling down her cheeks. Poor Kevin was in shock and wanted to cry but was fighting back the tears to be strong. They were all hurting so badly. The short time watching their reactions to Brian's death seemed like an eternity. I didn't know how to protect them from the pain they were experiencing.

As they settled down, we asked each of them if they wanted to go to the hospital to see Brian. All of them said they wanted to go without hesitation. We did not want to deprive them of seeing their big brother one last time, and so we started back to the hospital. The ride to the hospital was somber and surreal. How could this be happening to us?

We soon arrived at the emergency department, and we all went in as a family to see Brian's lifeless body lying there. The kids initially stared at him, but then slowly started towards him and began to touch his face. I think they were trying to make sure he was real, to convince themselves that this nightmare was actually happening and that this was actually Brian lying there. I could see the pain and agony in their eyes as they looked upon their brother lying there dead. Julie held her hand softly on his forehead and didn't want to leave him. Christie was a little more timid and wanted to stand by him but not constantly touch him, while Kevin continued to stare at Brian, not really knowing what to do or even feel.

Eventually our priest arrived, and we as a family—Cindy, Kevin, Julie, Christie, and myself—along with the priest, held hands in a circle around Brian and said the Lord's Prayer. The priest described Brian as having been on a mission here on earth which was now finished. He tried to ease my children's fears for Brian. He told them to think of their brother as walking to the edge of a cliff. With his mission completed here on earth, he had stepped over the edge. But instead of falling in terror, Brian had fallen into the comforting embrace of our Lord, safe and loved.

We said goodbye to our beloved Brian that night. In retrospect, I think having the kids see their brother that night gave each of them the chance to say goodbye and tell him one last time how much they loved him and would miss him. This was to be the start of a long, heart-wrenching healing process.

While Cindy took the kids back home, I waited with Brian until they came to take him to the morgue. I didn't want to leave him alone. I didn't want my little boy to be scared lying there all by himself. It was a horrible feeling, because as a parent you always want to protect your children from harm and from fear. You want to comfort them from all the dangers in this world. This was my last duty as Brian's father that night—to comfort him and keep him from being afraid. When they came to take him, I kissed his forehead one last time and told him that I loved him. My firstborn child, my oldest son, who will always be a part of me, was gone.

Chapter 2

A Beautiful Life

Life sometimes has a grotesque way of reminding us how fragile we are as human beings. If someone had told me that my son Brian would die at age 18 in an auto accident just four months before his high school graduation, I would have told them there's no way this could happen. But it did happen. We had a wonderful life once—me a neurosurgeon, my wife a forensic pathologist, and four smart, talented, beautiful children—the perfect family, really. Brian was the oldest of four, two boys and two girls, all with different interests and personalities. Kevin, our 15-year-old, is outgoing, confident, and somewhat mischievous. Julie, our 14-year-old, is quiet and reserved. Christie, our 11-year-old, is empathetic and sometimes overly sensitive. Then there was Brian, who was mature beyond his years.

There are so many things I would like to tell you about my son Brian so you could really get to know the amazing person he was. But how do you describe 18 years of life in such a short passage? Obviously you can't, but I will try to give you a synopsis of his character, personality, and the beautiful life he led.

There was a previous incident when I experienced terror and panic at the thought of losing Brian. We lived in Rochester, New York, where

Cindy and I were both in residency. It was a beautiful fall Saturday, and I had decided to go canoeing on the Erie Canal. I took along Brian, who was two years old, and a close friend, Paul, who was chief resident in Urology. The air was chilly, but the sun was shining. We wore long pants and heavy jackets, and I bundled up Brian so he would stay warm.

Before we left the dock, the rental person told us how safe the canoes were and how we couldn't tip them over if we tried. Paul didn't wear a life jacket, and I debated if Brian and I needed them, since we already had all our heavy clothes on. In addition, Paul and I were right there if anything happened. So we left the dock.

We canoed for several hours, paddling lazily along the Erie Canal. The turning leaves blazed in colors of burnt orange, yellow, and deep red. Only an occasional train horn or chirping of birds disrupted the stillness in the air. We were having a nice, relaxing afternoon, just the three of us.

At some point near the end of our trip, Brian spotted something in the water. As we leaned over to look, the canoe listed and, as if in slow motion, started to fill with water. The next thing I knew, Paul and I were in the water away from the canoe, and Brian was nowhere in sight. Since he was only two years old and could not swim, I immediately panicked. That sickening sensation filled the pit of my stomach with the thought that my child could be dead or dying, and there was nothing I could do about it.

The water was cold and murky, and Brian had vanished. I envisioned him struggling helplessly to reach the surface of the water but instead sinking to the bottom of the canal in his heavy clothes, dying a horrible death. We frantically dove under the water to try and find him. I could see nothing and felt blindly underwater in hopes of touching his body. *God, what have I done?* I thought.

What seemed like an eternity in actuality was a mere 30 or 40 seconds. Then it dawned on me to look under the canoe, which was overturned. We lifted it, and there was Brian, quietly shivering in the water under the canoe with his life jacket on.

You see, I did have Brian wear a life jacket that day, and it was the life jacket that saved his life. And to think that I had considered not putting it on him. Without it, Brian would have surely died at age two in the Erie Canal. But something had changed my mind at the last second, and I'd decided to put the life jacket on him.

It felt as if Brian had escaped death that day, and for the rest of his life I worried that something bad might happen to him. And it did. He lived 16 more years, then died tragically in a car accident.

I often wonder what made me change my mind that day about the life jacket. Was he meant to live for a purpose that he would fulfill in the next 16 years, only to be taken when he had fulfilled that purpose? I guess I will never know the answer to that question, but it sure does make me wonder.

~~~

From that point on, Brian lived a wonderful life. He was very active as a child and learned to play tennis, golf, football, baseball, basketball, table tennis, and chess. He learned to bowl, run track, ice-skate, snow ski, water-ski, snowboard, wakeboard, scuba dive, and play Spikeball. He loved sports and was active in all of them. He also loved watching them on TV. He and Kevin spent endless hours watching ESPN together, and he and I spent hours watching golf together. We loved to watch golf tournaments, particularly the Masters each year. Golf was our way of bonding with each other.

The summer before he died, he had the opportunity to play in the Optimist International golf tournament at the PGA National golf course in Palm Beach, Florida, a professional course designed by Jack Nicklaus, where the touring pros play the Honda Classic each year. Afterward, Brian was so looking forward to watching the pros play on the same holes that he had played on. Unfortunately, he never made it to spring to watch the tournament. I watched it for him on TV and cried as I remembered following him around each of those same holes for several days during the last summer of his life.

Then there were the trips and family vacations. Brian was lucky enough to travel many times to some pretty fun places. He had been to Disney World and on a Disney cruise as a child to meet Mickey Mouse. He had scuba dived multiple times in the blue waters of the Caribbean to see exotic fish and sea turtles, which he often chased after. At Niagara Falls he rode the *Maid of the Mist* to the base of the falls and walked behind the falls themselves. At Vail, Snowbird, and Keystone ski resorts he skied and snowboarded down mountains, went high-speed tubing, and rode in an authentic horse-drawn sleigh through the open snow fields of Colorado. In New York City he saw the lights at Christmas, visited the Statue of Liberty, and went to the top of the Empire State Building. In Denver he hiked up a mountain and watched a Nuggets NBA game. In Costa Rica he saw an active volcano, went whitewater rafting, hiked in the rainforest, and zip-lined through the canopy. In Jamaica he rode horseback on the beach, rafted down a canopied river in the mountains, and swam with dolphins. In Mexico he explored underground cenotes and an enormous natural outdoor water park called Xcaret.

He road-tripped to Florida with his family, fought in the car with his siblings, and searched for shells on the beach. He stayed up all night with his family at Cape Canaveral to watch the space shuttle lift off at dawn and met a real-life astronaut. He took boat rides on Lake Erie to the islands and visited Cedar Point Amusement Park each summer. At our cottage he water-skied, wakeboarded, and spent time with his family and cousins.

At home he played basketball in the driveway, hung out with friends in our basement, and ice-skated and played hockey on our homemade ice rink. He watched movies with us at home and went out to dinner with us as a family. And he joined us on our last family vacation, a Caribbean cruise, just one month before he died. It was just the six of us, our last time together as a family. What a wonderful life he lived in just 18 short years—a life filled with so much love and precious memories to last most people a lifetime.

Another big part of Brian's life was his love for animals, particularly his dogs. From the time he was a baby to the day he died, he always had the companionship of a dog. Our first dog was Coco, a chocolate Lab, which we got the year before Brian was born. We spent many hours taking her for walks or swimming at our local parks in Rochester, New York. On the weekends, we often went to a place called Taughannock Falls, which was a river tributary feeding into a finger lake, where we walked Coco up the riverbed to the falls and let her swim in the natural pool at the base of the falls. The excitement and fear in Brian's eyes when Coco swam near the falls was precious. He would yell and yell for her to swim back, terrified that she would disappear under the falls. Coco moved back to Toledo with us and lived a long, happy life. We eventually got a black Lab as well, which we named Nautica. Oh, the fun Brian had playing ball with those two dogs.

Coco died at age 13, when Brian was 12. He was heartbroken, as were our other children. Coco had been there his whole life, and now she was gone. This was Brian's first real encounter with death. We have had several other dogs through the years and currently have Nautica and Ellie, a Springer Spaniel. Whenever Brian came home from school or after a workout, he greeted his dogs with loving enthusiasm, a trait that he will always be remembered for.

Then there was golf. The kid could golf, and what a passion he had for it. In just four short years he became an accomplished golfer, achieving a 4 handicap. He played in numerous tournaments, both in state and out of state. I remember the first time Brian ever swung a golf club. I took him and Kevin for a golf lesson at the Sylvania Country Club where we were members. Brian was in eighth grade. I sat on the top of the hill at the far end of the driving range and watched how well both Brian and Kevin made contact with the ball for their first time ever swinging a club.

After that first lesson, Brian's passion for golf quickly grew. He began to study the game and play on a regular basis. One summer at SCC, he played the second most rounds of any member, second only to a retired physician. As Brian continued to play, I watched him grow and mature as a person, learning life lessons about himself—about his capabilities, limitations, and most importantly, failures. Everyone wants to win, but Brian learned that winning wasn't always possible. He also quickly learned that he could only have a chance at winning if he became better at the game, and he could only get better at the game if he practiced. And so he did. It was no different than academics. If he didn't put in the time and effort, he would not make the grade.

But something I noticed developing in Brian was his ability to accept his limitations and failures and learn from them. When he shot a bad score, he didn't give up. Instead, he practiced that much harder to achieve a better score the next time. He was learning about balance in life. If he didn't play well on any given day, he knew that he had given it his all and moved on. He did not dwell on his failures.

In time, he gained an understanding that life is not just about winning or being the best. It is about setting goals and being content that you gave it your all no matter what the outcome. If only we could all learn to accept our failures. That is the true measure of a person. It is easy to acknowledge one's accomplishments, but the true test is to acknowledge one's shortcomings. That means accepting yourself for who you are and not what you think others want you to be.

Brian seemed to understand that life was about appreciating what he had and using his fortunate situation to encourage and help others—to be humble and help pass his talents and knowledge on to others. In golf, Brian often tried to help other players in little ways, like checking yardages for them with his range finder during tournaments or raking sand traps to keep the pace of play moving. On the golf team, he frequently shared his talents with his junior teammates and took the time to help them improve their game. He was competitive, yet comfortable with himself to the point that he did not have to worry about losing an advantage to other players by helping them.

He demonstrated a similar demeanor in the realm of academics. A brief story follows to illustrate this point. A student in Brian's class at St. John's Jesuit High School recently told me that Brian had prepared an extensive set of notes for an open-book exam they were taking in history class. On the morning of the exam, Brian copied all of his notes and shared the notes with the whole class. Of course, this was done without the teacher's knowledge. The entire class scored well on the test. He always strived to achieve high grades, but for his own satisfaction. He didn't worry if someone was going to outdo him; he was more concerned with whether he could outdo himself. Brian was gaining an understanding that life was not all about what he wanted as an individual, but much more about helping others get what they wanted.

Life was also about satisfaction and confidence in oneself. As his golf game improved, he became more confident in himself, and with confidence came maturity as well as better scores. His best round was a 68 at Heather Downs Country Club, but the round he was most proud of was the 69 he shot at the historic Inverness Country Club, which has hosted four US Opens, two PGA Championships, and two Senior PGA Championships. He shot this score, which is two under par, at age 17 from the gold tees, which measure 6,800 yards. I was there with him that day, along with his younger brother Kevin. I saw the excitement in his eyes. He was happy, alive, and full of energy on that beautiful, sunny day. He was confident and proud that he had reached another goal in his life.

To give a summary of what Brian had learned in life thus far would be impossible, but I can give you a real-life example of the person he was becoming. He once told me about a time when he pulled up next to an older car at a stoplight. An adult sat in the driver's seat, and Brian thought to himself, *Who am I to be driving a nicer car than this grownup next to me?*

I don't think that I have ever been any prouder of him than at that moment, because I realized he got it. He appreciated how fortunate he was. He understood that there were more important things in life than what he wanted or what he already had. I think this is part of Brian's legacy: to take what you have, appreciate it, try to master it, and then pass it on to others.

Then there was his education. Academics were always foremost among Brian's priorities, the crux of his disciplined life and a solidifying theme which defined his character and drive for success. From an early age, Brian was an overachiever scholastically. He was a straight-A student throughout grade school, junior high, and high school. He maintained a 4.5 GPA in high school and scored a 32 on his ACT. He wanted to go to college with the intent of eventually becoming an orthodontist. He was accepted to Ohio State University, the University of Miami, Michigan State, and the University of North Carolina-Chapel Hill at the time of his death. He had not yet heard from UCLA, the University of Michigan, or the University of Florida.

I have no doubt that he would have achieved his goal of being an orthodontist if he had continued to pursue that particular goal, because if I can say one thing about Brian, it's that when he set his mind to do something, he did not give up until he had achieved it. When he wanted to learn how to juggle, he researched the concept on the Internet, and within a weekend's time, he was an accomplished juggler. He was eventually able to juggle four balls without difficulty. When he wanted to solve the Rubik's cube, he got on the Internet, watched a video, and mastered it in an afternoon. There was a time in eighth grade when he wanted to get all 100 percent grades for a quarter. He challenged himself and did it. The boy was smart and self-motivated, both traits that served him well in life. You see, most anyone can achieve goals with motivation and hard work, but it is discipline you have to develop and commit to. Brian quickly learned that he could achieve most things by living his life with this philosophy in mind.

I write of Brian's interests, achievements, and drive for success with the hope that many of you will read this and encourage your children to strive for great things. Tell them about Brian and what he accomplished. Tell them he was a kid just like them with hopes, dreams, and desires of going to college, having a family of his own, and living a long, happy life. Tell them about his beautiful life and how it can all be lost in an instant. Make them understand that every day of your life counts for so much more than you think, because tomorrow may never come.

Today is the first day of the rest of your life. So set a goal and work toward that goal every day, even if just for a little bit, until you achieve it. Take what talents you may have to offer the world, learn to appreciate and build confidence in those talents, become a master of your talents, and then pass your legacy on to others. This is what life is all about: taking your particular talents and using them for the betterment of others. I think Brian was starting to understand that concept.

As I reflect back on what I have written so far, it makes me realize what a beautiful life Brian had and what a wonderful life we had with Brian in it. With him gone, our lives will never be the same. There will always be an emptiness where there used to be joy and happiness. Please keep this in mind as you read on, and never lose sight of how much you are loved by the people who surround you.

Chapter 3

Life Without Brian: Day One

I walked alone out of the emergency department around 3:30 a.m. after kissing Brian goodbye for the last time. I rode home with my two brothers and can't even remember if we spoke a word during the drive. The car was cold, and I was numb.

At home, I found my wife and three children sitting together on the couch quietly in the dark. I sat down next to them, thinking, *What do we do now?* The most heinous thing that could have possibly happened was now a reality. Our child was dead.

Exhausted, we went upstairs to bed. I wanted us to all be together that night as a family, so Christie and Julie slept in our bed. I asked Kevin if he wanted to sleep on the floor with me in our bedroom, but he said no. I told him we could grab some sleeping bags from the basement and lie on the floor next to Mom and the girls, but he shook his head. I felt so bad for him but didn't know how to comfort him any better. I will never know exactly why he didn't want to sleep with us, but I suspect he wanted to be close to his big brother Brian. You see, Kevin's bedroom is immediately next to Brian's, and the headboards of their beds are back-to-back, although separated by the bedroom wall. He wanted to be next to Brian's room that night, the night of his brother's death. So I went to his room with him and said good night for the first time without Brian in his life. Since Brian's death, I have found that every experience seems to be a new experience which I define in relationship to the death of my child.

Nautica, our black Lab, who always sleeps upstairs by the kids' rooms, would not come upstairs. She stayed down by the garage door entrance that night, waiting for Brian to come home.

We didn't sleep much that first night, but tried to close our eyes on and off. The continual thoughts about what had happened were all-encompassing. We all arose shortly thereafter, as Julie had an early-morning basketball game. I couldn't believe that just hours after seeing Brian lying dead at the hospital, we were going to a basketball game, but I'm so glad we did. I know this meant a lot to Julie, because she and her team were playing the game for her big brother Brian. But there was another reason she didn't want to miss this game. Her coach had told her the day before to get a good night's sleep, because they really needed her for the game. She had told Brian what the coach said, and Brian had told her, "Doesn't that make you feel good that your coach wants you at the game?" Julie felt good about her big brother's words and would not consider missing the game.

Parents came up to us and gave their condolences. It was so surreal, as if they weren't talking about our son. How could they be talking about Brian, who had been alive just hours before?

The game was very emotional for both teams, with all of the girls crying at some point. We led most of the game, but in the end, Julie's team lost by two points.

After the game ended, we came home and sat in our empty, silent house. The aura of Brian's death was everywhere, and it was stifling. I couldn't sit still and began to pace around the house. I didn't know what to do. I was uneasy with the world, this horrible new world without Brian in it. I didn't know how to fix this problem or make it better. I asked Brian over and over why he had to die, as though he could somehow answer me and make it all better. What had he ever done to deserve to die a tragic death at such a young age? He was a good boy with a very giving heart. Nothing made sense to me.

Later that morning, a friend called and asked if a group of parents could come over to say hi. We were hesitant, but at the same time needed the company of others. Around noon, the first of our friends started to arrive. Three hundred people must have passed through our house that day. Friends from out of town and even different states arrived to support us.

All of Brian's friends came over. They wanted to be in the house, which offered a direct connection to Brian. They went to his room, where they sat and cried. All his personal belongings lay as he had left them the day before. This was the most tangible spot left in the world, where his presence could be felt in the way he had left his room organized—the way he had lined his shoes up under his bed; the spot next to his bathroom where he left his backpack the day before; his personal belongings arranged on the night table next to his bed. All served as reminders of who Brian was. Other kids went to the basement, where they had spent so much time together having fun, listening to music, playing table tennis and pool, and talking about their lives and plans for the day and the future. They lingered for what seemed like hours, as if their presence might bring him back.

I felt the same way much of that day. I can never describe in words the magnitude of pain, as well as the love that was present in our home that day! I assume it is the universal bond between a parent and a child that brought us all so close together. Each of the parents at our house knew that it could have easily been one of their children who had died. I was told that quite a few parents held their children a little closer that night. Everyone seemed to gain a better appreciation for life and how abruptly it can end.

That evening, there was a vigil at the high school that the kids put together in Brian's memory. Their turnabout dance, which Brian was to attend that night, was canceled. Everyone brought their corsages to our house in remembrance of Brian. There must have been 300 people in attendance. Very nice things were said about Brian, all with a sense of disbelief that something of this nature could happen to such a nice young man.

I remember one comment in particular made by one of his best friends. Brian had recently moved to Ottawa Hills High School after three years at St. John's Jesuit High School. He had been at Ottawa Hills for only five months. It was an extremely tough decision for Brian to move to a new high school, particularly in his senior year. But the switch was something he really wanted to do, and he had done it well. He had transitioned into the school seamlessly and into the student body without any problems and quickly made friends, which I could see by the number of people he invited over to our house on a regular basis, the kids who stopped over to pick him up to go out for the afternoon or evening, and the friends who stopped over to play Spikeball in our backyard, even if Brian wasn't here. He was enjoying his newfound friendships and exciting new social life at OHHS.

During the vigil that night, his friend spoke about how quickly Brian had made friends. What touched me most deeply was what followed. He said, "Kids who move to a new school usually need to try to fit in with everyone else. But with Brian, that was not the case. We tried to fit in with him and be more like he was."

At that moment, I think most people began to cry if they weren't already doing so. I can think of no greater honor or tribute from one friend to another. I wish my son could have been there to hear what his friend said and witness the emotions overcoming a community in Brian's honor. It was a testament to how Brian had affected so many people's lives in such a short period of time.

Once the comments had ended, a procession of cars was underway to the crash site where Brian's life had been taken less than 24 hours earlier. His car had struck a large, majestic oak sitting alone off the side of the road, next to the edge of the woods. The tree itself was barely scratched, yet Brian's car was demolished. This old, unforgiving tree was the only real witness to my son's death.

Hundreds of people showed up along this gently curving, snow-covered road. What an odd feeling to want to see where someone has died. It may sound creepy, but again, I think it served as a tangible place where people could embrace or sense him, or imagine his last living moments on this earth. It was the last concrete tie to Brian before he passed to the next world and became intangible to us. To many, that tree will always represent Brian's gravesite, because that is where he died.

My hope is that the tree will come to represent so much more. I hope it will serve as a reminder of life, to help people pause and reflect on how fragile and precious life is, to imagine for a moment waking up one morning to find out their son or daughter is dead and they will never have the chance to see him or her alive again. Would you have done anything differently? Do you feel comfortable that they knew you loved them? Did you tell them enough that you loved them, what a great kid they were, and how proud you were of their accomplishments in life? Do you think they knew all of this, or would you need a second chance?

Second chances rarely come our way, and for Brian, there was no second chance. For me and my family, there is no second chance to tell Brian how much we loved him and how proud we were of him. I have to believe he knew this, but I can only hope. I also hope that a tragedy of this nature will serve as a catalyst for people to reevaluate what is truly important in their lives and prevent any regrets they may harbor if a loved one dies unexpectedly.

Lastly, and probably most importantly, I hope Brian's death serves as a stark reminder of all the wonderful things in our lives that we take for granted every day—a reminder to appreciate what we have, especially our children, to tell them how proud we are of them and of their accomplishments, to encourage them to believe in themselves, and as Brian would say, "Just be you!" To tell our kids how much we love them, because in a heartbeat, we may lose that chance forever when tomorrow never comes and we are left only with a feeling of regret.

I found a quote of Brian's that he posted on Twitter:

Sometimes I wish there was no tomorrow. Think of how much fun we could have today.

He posted that on December 28, 2012, at 8:56 a.m., the morning of his 18th birthday. Brian had a great passion for life, an extremely positive attitude, and a love for generating infectious enthusiasm in others. I hope the legacy of his death will continue to instill these qualities in others as he did in life.

Chapter 4

The Aftermath

Our first day after Brian's death ended with our return home from the crash site to face the aloneness of our first full night without Brian. This is the time when all activity ceases, and we are left to face the haunting memories of a lifetime. The girls slept in their rooms, and Kevin in his. Cindy and I lay quietly in our bed, holding each other inconsolably and crying silently through the night. The night seemed like an eternity as we waited for daybreak, because we knew in the morning that we had to do the unthinkable: plan our son's funeral. What a horrible thing for any parent to have to do.

I called Jim Bolander, our funeral director, to make arrangements for Brian's funeral. Brian was to have his funeral at Hoeflinger Funeral Home and be buried at Calvary Cemetery next to my parents and grandparents. My great-grandfather Michael Hoeflinger established the funeral home in 1875 after having moved from Germany as a cabinetmaker. Everyone in our family who has passed has been buried by Hoeflinger Funeral Home, and now it was Brian's turn.

Jim has worked for the funeral home since I was a young boy, and he knows our family extremely well. I remember him walking through our front door that day and the feeling I had when I first saw him at our house. I began to cry as I looked into his eyes and saw the pain he was experiencing, not only for us but for himself. It was the same pain I had seen in his eyes 10 years earlier when my dad died, and 25 years earlier when my mom died. I couldn't talk. I could only feel the indescribable desire to tell myself that this was not happening and that Brian was not dead.

We sat down at the kitchen table, and Jim described in detail what needed to be done. Cindy would not sit with us for most of that time, as I don't think she could bear the thought of what was happening. He asked when we wanted to have the showings and how long we wanted them to last, what type of flowers we wanted to be placed on Brian's casket, and what church we would have the service in. We also needed to write an obituary and pick out the casket.

Much of this was a blur, but I remember picking out the casket. As I looked through a book of caskets, I kept asking myself how this could be happening. I did not want to pick one, but knew I must. I finally picked a casket with a cherry-wood finish and golf-related inserts on each corner. The silhouette of a golfer standing on a green was inlaid on the fabric of the door that was to close forever over Brian's upper body, as an everlasting reminder to him of the game he had loved so much.

There is no way to put into words how it felt picking out my son's casket. It is a feeling that I would never wish upon anybody.

In a soft voice, Jim asked us to start thinking about which clothes we wanted Brian to be buried in and which personal items we wanted to put in the casket with him. We hadn't had to pick clothes out for Brian since he was a little boy. He always liked looking nice, and people noticed. The boy had done his own laundry since seventh grade. That was how much his clothes meant to him and how much he cared about how he looked. Shortly before we left on our last family vacation together, we had gone shopping at the mall. Brian and I bought these pullover sweaters, different colors of course, but the same sweater. He wore this sweater all the time. It reminded me so much of Brian and our last loving memories as a family on our final vacation together. We knew we wanted him to be buried in this.

Finally, there was writing the obituary, a job I had been involved with only once before when my dad died 10 years earlier. This felt different. I would be writing about my son, who was only 18 years old. I didn't want to think about the task of writing his obituary, hoping somehow it would go away. I wanted to be a child again and have my parents take care of everything. But I was the parent now, and it was our job as Brian's parents to write this last entry for him to let people know who he was and what he had left behind in this world. We spent days performing this arduous chore, but the final outcome was just right.

All the while, people continued to visit. Our kids went about their business as their friends came in and out of the house. As each afternoon faded and evening came, things quieted down, people left, and again we were alone in the silence of our house to endure another night of agonizing loneliness and pain. Even though Cindy and the kids were there, I felt so alone and empty inside, as if no one could ever reach me in this desolate place I was in. I didn't sleep for the next three nights.

The days of showing Brian's body at the funeral home were long and hard. Cindy and I stood for 12 hours each day, greeting person after person as each paid their last respects to Brian. More than 600 people passed through the doors each day, waiting in line for up to three hours to see Brian and talk to us. Jim told us that more people had come to see Brian in those two days than any other in the 138-year history of the funeral home. We had mementos of Brian's life on display for people to see as they waited in line—photos, trophies, grades, and accomplishments demonstrating what an amazing young man he was. We had spent hours agonizing over which personal belongings and pictures to bring to the funeral home so everything would be just perfect. This was our last chance to show people who Brian was and what a wonderful life he had led.

The funeral was on Friday, one week after his death. I remember watching my family say their final goodbyes before the casket would be closed forever. The kids and I had written letters to Brian, which the girls placed in the casket next to him. I was the last to say goodbye before the final closing of the casket. I gazed at him, wishing this moment would never end. I couldn't bear the thought of never seeing my son again. One last time, I told him how much I loved him and how very proud I had always been of him. I told him that I would see him again in heaven one day.

Then the casket was sealed forever.

As a family, we walked behind the casket as it was wheeled to the front of the church, which was filled to capacity both upstairs and downstairs, with well over 1,000 people inside. The homily was performed by Father Weirzel, who had known Brian well since grade school.

"Brian loved to clap for others," he said during the service. "I wonder if anyone ever clapped for him." Father Weirzel knew the unique talent that Brian possessed for clapping. Brian could cup his hands and clap them against any surface to produce an amazingly loud sound. His talent was coined by his friends as "the clap."

Now Father Weirzel began to clap for Brian, and the entire church full of people joined in. The sound was deafening. What an overwhelming show of love for Brian this was! I hoped he was watching and clapping along with us.

The procession to the cemetery was given a police escort, and police blocked intersection after intersection just for Brian. The whole day felt surreal, like a chapter in a book that I was reading about someone else's life, rather than my own.

At the gravesite, after the final prayer, we released five white doves into the air, one for each of us, to symbolize releasing Brian's spirit to heaven and God. As I watched my children each release a bird, I felt a sense of relief that we had put Brian to rest. Now was the time to face the remainder of our lives without Brian.

I was not sure I could do it. I felt like I would never be able to return to work. I needed to be with my family and at home, where Brian had lived. To honor Brian, I needed to make something positive come from this tragedy. But more than this, there was a special kind of energy that had been associated with Brian's death, an outpouring of love far beyond what anyone could have anticipated.

Here is a personal comment sent to us after Brian's death which exemplifies the effect of his death on so many others:

I never knew Brian. However, as a former resident of Ottawa Hills, I have had a constant stream of messages, pictures, and statuses describing how amazing he was. I have talked with family and friends, some who knew him and some who did not, and everyone seems affected in some way. I have found myself crying and mourning with the rest of Ottawa Hills the last couple of days, because although I never knew Brian, somehow, I still feel like I lost someone. I am deeply sorry for your loss and have been praying a lot. But despite the sorrow, I cannot help but notice that this tragedy has ignited a life, an energy, a movement to this village and everyone connected to it. I have never seen anything like it. He really must have been something special. Stay strong and know people are thinking of you, near and far.

Brian's death brought together people across many communities and different age groups to share in a common sense of loss, as well as a sense of life—all-important life that binds us together as human beings. When that life is lost, it is a reminder of how fragile our lives are and how quickly they can be taken from us. It was this overwhelming energy of humanity that spread beyond the confines of Brian's physical death which I knew I had to tap into, turning a tragedy into a positive outcome for others. Thus started the creation of Brian's memorial fund and golf tournaments.

Chapter 5

A Life Shaped By Tragedy

As I think back on my own life, there have been many events, including tragic ones, that have shaped me into who I am today. I am the middle child of five, with two older brothers and a younger sister and brother. I grew up in a middle-income family in an average neighborhood. We lived in a three-bedroom ranch home with seven of us. My two older brothers and myself shared a single room.

I have very fond memories of my early childhood. There were lots of kids in our neighborhood and lots of things to do. As a young boy, I spent most of my time outside swimming, playing baseball and football, riding my bike, and exploring the local woods. There were so many adventures to be had as a child playing outside, which kids today don't seem to appreciate. On the other hand, the world is a different place today than it was 40 years ago when I was a child. In the winter, we built snow forts, ice-skated and played hockey, built snowmen, and had snowball fights. I had a paper route and delivered newspapers after school every day of the year. I did this from fourth through seventh grade.

When I started high school, I knew most of the kids in my grade, as I had gone to school with them in the past. Then, during the latter part of my freshman year of high school, our family moved to Florida. Moving to a new state meant losing all my old friends and having to make new ones. It was a frightening thought, but I had no choice in the matter.

We moved into a nice neighborhood, and I made friends fairly quickly. But making new friends meant fitting in with their way of life. To fit in and be accepted in this area meant indulging in drugs and alcohol—and so I did. What else could I do, since all of my new friends were doing it, right? For months, marijuana and alcohol became an integral part of my social life. All were easily accessible, and everyone I knew was doing it. It seemed harmless for a while, until my grades began to fall and I could see that I was going nowhere. The interesting thing is that my parents did not seem to notice what was happening to me. Being a typical teenager, I didn't approach my parents with this problem and took it on alone.

Eventually, one Saturday morning after a Friday night of partying, I awoke feeling as if I was going to die. I was sweating and shaking, and my heart was racing and pounding. I did not know what was happening to me. This feeling was so unsettling that I immediately knew what I had to do: stop the alcohol and drugs.

For the rest of that weekend, I lay low. When my friends called, I told them I was sick. When Monday came around and I went to school, I told my friends that I still wanted to spend time with them, but I no longer wanted to be involved in their "recreational" activities.

You can probably guess what happened next. My so-called friends dropped me like a hot potato. From that day forth, my previous group of friends would no longer associate with me or even talk to me. If I approached them, they just walked away. They ignored me in the halls at school and on the streets in our neighborhood.

My life changed drastically in one day. I had lost all of my friends over that one statement. I began eating lunch alone at school and frequently sat by myself. I avoided social gatherings so I wouldn't be publicly ostracized and ignored by my previous set of friends. I began spending more time by myself and often went fishing alone or treasure hunting on the beach with the metal detector I had bought. I was feeling insecure with myself and with my place in the world. Yet in a strange way, I felt more confident than ever because I had made a decision, the right decision, to stand up for what I believed and not give in to what others wanted.

Peer pressure is extremely tough to deal with, but it can be overcome if you stay true to yourself. You have to value yourself more than you value what others think of you.

As time went on, I eventually made a new subset of friends and became a very different person as a result. A stimulus is always required to bring about change. But you have to commit to that change and not waver. The road is often hard but is certainly travelable with persistence. I was willing to lose all of my friends to stand by what I believed in, and I did. It was absolutely not easy for me, but most things worthwhile in life are not easy. Doing the right thing is usually the more difficult path to take. Everyone is able to make a choice; you just have to decide who you are making the choice for. Is it for yourself, or is it to please others? Always stay true to yourself, and in the end, you will go far. Never let others influence you toward what you know to be wrong.

Most of the time, people who try to influence you to do something such as drinking are themselves insecure and will try to pull you into their situation to make themselves feel more comfortable and secure about themselves. A truly confident person does not need to sway others into their way of thinking or need to influence others to enhance their own self-worth.

~~~

Three years of high school went by in Florida, and I can honestly say that I have very few fond memories of school during this period. My family moved back to Toledo near the end of high school, but I stayed with my grandparents in Florida. I had been working at a gas station after school for years and had a life where I was, so I opted not to move back. I had actually signed up at the University of South Florida for fall classes to become a marine biologist. I loved the outdoors and had always loved the water and scuba diving. I became a certified diver in 1981.

During that first summer after high school, I received a call one morning from my mom to tell me that my brother Eric had been involved in a horrible car accident. He was 21 years old at the time and a junior in college at the University of Toledo. He had suffered a severe head injury and had undergone emergency brain surgery in the middle of the night, but the neurosurgeon said that Eric would most likely die.

I flew home to Toledo that day. It was the first time I had ever flown on a plane. I was 18 at the time. I went straight to the hospital and saw my brother Eric lying there in the intensive care unit in a coma, his entire head bandaged and a monitoring device sticking out of his upper forehead. His face was grotesquely bruised and swollen, and he in no way looked like my brother. A breathing tube protruded from his mouth, and chest tubes stuck out of both sides of his chest.

I watched the numbers associated with his brain monitor and prayed for the pressure in his brain to stay low. The neurosurgeon stopped by once a day, usually in the early morning or late in the evening, to examine Eric. He reiterated the severity of Eric's injury and told our family that he didn't think Eric would survive. If he did survive, he probably would remain in a coma. I wondered how something like this could happen to my brother. What had he ever done to deserve this?

I stayed in Toledo for at least two weeks and went to the hospital every day to be with my family. We practically lived there and would wait all day just to hear a few minutes' update from the neurosurgeon on Eric's condition. We hung on his every word, hoping that he would give us some ray of hope and tell us that Eric would be okay again. As I spent my days and nights in and around the neurointensive care unit, I became intrigued by the environment of Eric's care and the thought of becoming a neurosurgeon. This tragic exposure to the world of neurosurgery, at least the small part of it I was able to see, changed my perspective of the future.

I returned to my grandparents' house in Florida, but soon knew what I needed to do: move back to Toledo to be close to my family. I canceled the classes I had signed up for at the University of South Florida and gave up my dream of being a marine biologist. I now had a new dream: to be a neurosurgeon. Back home, I signed up for classes at the University of Toledo with the intent of going to medical school and hopefully one day becoming a neurosurgeon.

Eric survived and remained in a coma for six months. He gradually awoke, but the process was painfully slow. He never regained his independence. The injury to his brain had left him paralyzed on his right side and prevented him from ever walking or talking again. He has required constant care and communicates only by spelling words out on a letter board. It's painful to remember the vibrant, motivated person he used to be and see him turned into an invalid requiring care from others with no true meaningful interaction with the world. His whole life and future plans were taken away in a moment by a tragic car accident.

Eric lived in a rehab and nursing home for many years but did eventually make it home. My mother devoted all of her energy and essentially the remainder of her life to Eric's care. I watched the pain she went through over the horrible injury her child had suffered. I'll always remember her telling me that there was no greater pain in life for a parent than that associated with the injury of a child. She and our family were never the same after his injury.

I finished four years of college and entered medical school, all while my mom continued to care for Eric. In her free time, she wrote letters to her friends. She loved to write letters. One morning in the early fall of 1990, during my second year of medical school, I noticed my mom having trouble writing with her right hand. When I asked her how long she had had this problem, she answered about two weeks. I could see she was scared but didn't want to let on about her concern. While in medical school, I had learned enough thus far to know that something was quite wrong. I had kept in touch with Eric's neurosurgeon, who was an attending physician at my medical school, and called him to tell him about my mom. He had me bring her to the hospital that day for a

CT scan of her brain. She knew something must be very wrong and was scared.

The results were the worst. The CT scan showed at least 10 masses in her brain. My mom had diffuse metastatic brain cancer, which was terminal and a certain death sentence.

We did not tell her the results of the CT scan immediately. She was admitted to the hospital directly from the ER and started on steroids, which helped with her hand weakness. I stayed with my mom until late that night and then went home, in sheer disbelief that this was happening. I will always remember the feeling I had the next morning when I awoke and wished so very badly that yesterday had all been a terrible dream and that my mom was fine. It was like a nightmare that I could not wake up from. I felt utterly helpless.

The next morning I arrived at the hospital to find my mother crying alone in the darkness of her hospital room. She told me the neurosurgeon had stopped by late last night after I had left and told her that she had malignant brain cancer. I felt so bad that she had been all alone with no family present when she learned of this horrible news. I never forgot that experience, and to this day as a neurosurgeon and a doctor, I have never told a patient news of that nature without a family member being present.

At some point during my mother's hospital stay, the possibility of multiple brain abscesses was brought up as a diagnosis. As a family, we immediately began hoping and praying it was an infection that could be treated with antibiotics, rather than cancer. This false hope was short-lived. My mom underwent a brain biopsy shortly thereafter, confirming the diagnosis of malignant cancer. She underwent a full metastatic workup, but no primary source of her cancer was ever found.

She underwent two brain surgeries, chemotherapy, and radiation treatment to her brain. All her hair fell out, and she was often violently ill from the treatment. I watched her condition quickly deteriorate as time went on. The day came when I was talking to my mom and she was no longer making sense. I started to cry, because at that moment I knew that my mom was gone and I could never have her back again.

We brought her home, and soon thereafter we stopped all treatment and medication. I watched her quickly deteriorate. We no longer fed her, as she could no longer swallow food or liquids. She soon slipped into a coma and died within days, just three months after the initial diagnosis was made. She was 62.

I was alone next to my mother when she died. I watched her take her last breath as I stood by helplessly. I started to cry as I ran to the kitchen to tell my dad. I wanted him to make everything better, but I knew he could not. I was devastated. How would I live without my mother?

At the age of 25, I now faced the harsh reality that I no longer had a mother in this world. I felt lost. My mom and I had always had a special bond, and now, with her gone, I felt empty and alone inside. My wife to be, Cindy, and I had been dating for about four months, so my mom did have the chance to meet her but would not have the chance to be at our wedding or meet any of her grandchildren.

With the passing of my mother and my continued interaction with the same neurosurgeon who had treated both my brother and my mother, I felt more committed to becoming a neurosurgeon than ever before. After medical school, I was accepted to the University of

Rochester neurosurgery program. Cindy and I had married, and she would also begin her residency in pathology at Strong Memorial Hospital, where I was to train as well. After seven years of residency and three children later, I graduated from training, and we moved back to Toledo to take up practice, me as a neurosurgeon and Cindy as a forensic pathologist.

While I had been focused on my training for seven years, my grandmother in Toledo had devoted her life to taking care of Eric. She died during my time in residency. In addition, the grandparents I had lived with in Florida and had spent so many happy times with both died as well. My father took over the task of caring for Eric and devoted his remaining years to Eric's well-being.

My father lived for four years after I moved back home to Toledo. Cindy and I had our last child, Christie, during that time. I watched my father gradually slow down over those four years, and near the end, he could barely walk due to shortness of breath. He had been a heavy smoker since he was a teenager. I had spent most of my life in school to become a neurosurgeon and was finally home and able to spend time with my father, but now his health was declining and he could no longer do many of the activities we once enjoyed together. For example, I loved to golf, but physically he could no longer do it. It was a sad feeling to spend my life working toward a goal and at the same time lose out on another aspect of my life—my time with my father. I remember such good times when I was a young boy spending time with my dad, being on vacation and fishing on Lake Erie with him in the early morning, just the two of us before the other kids woke up, taking an occasional day trip with him when he had business out of town, going swimming with him in our backyard pool, and all the times he had driven us to Ann Arbor to go sledding and teach us how to ski—all fond memories of a father who had grown old while I was making my way in the world.

I vividly remember the morning he died. My dad had not been feeling well lately, and I had invited him to spend the week at my house. Eric now lived in a nursing home because my dad could no longer take care of him. During this week, I was able to enjoy his company one last time. We watched TV together each evening after I came home from work or simply talked about the day's events. We had a small glass of port wine each evening, which he so loved. He had a chance to spend time with Cindy and his grandchildren. He had a chance to really get to know Brian, Kevin, Julie, and Christie. I was extremely lucky to have spent this last week of his life as we did.

The morning of his death, I was operating at St. Luke's Hospital when Cindy called to tell me my dad was not doing well. She had called an ambulance to take him to the ER. I had finished my first surgery and canceled my next. I drove home and arrived to see my father being carried out on a stretcher to the ambulance. We followed the ambulance to the hospital, where my father was admitted to the ER. Tests were quickly ordered, and then we waited.

I will never forget the last thing my father said to me. I was in the room alone with him, and he turned to me and said, "I'm so tired, Brian. I'd like to take a quick nap."

I said, "Why don't you sleep, Dad?" and he closed his eyes. Within moments, his heart monitor turned to a V-tach rhythm. No one was in the room with us. I felt for a pulse, and there was none. I started chest compressions on my father. ER personnel quickly arrived and took over. After several minutes, there was no response. I looked at my dad's eyes and saw that they were fixed and dilated. I knew he was gone, so I told them to stop treatment. I did not want him to be revived at this point, only to become a vegetable.

My dad died on April 8, 2003, four days before his 77th birthday. I was 38 years old, and my father was dead. I was there alone with my dad the moment he died, as I had been with my mother so many years before. For the first time in my life, I was without a parent, and I felt a horrible aloneness. With both parents now gone, I felt like an orphan. It was the moment of realization that I had now become my parents, and my children were now me. I could never be a child again.

At this point, I figured that I had experienced my share of loss, sorrow, and tragedy—enough to last me the rest of my life. Then came Brian's death 10 years later. He had just turned 18, and I was 48.

Does it ever end? I wonder. Tragedy and death have forged such a big part of who I am as a person. But when is enough? When does it become detrimental and no longer a normal part of growing up into adulthood?

The death of our son has taken an enormous toll on Cindy and myself. Our lives feel ruined and all happiness gone. We will never be the same people we were before our son died. I can function day to day in an effective manner, but I look forward to nothing and live without the enthusiasm that I used to have for life before Brian died. I'm sure our remaining children have noticed our change, and this will be a part of their growing process on the road to becoming adults.

I briefly tell you of these sorrowful events to exemplify how life experiences can be used to the benefit of others. As a neurosurgeon and as a human being, I use these life experiences to relate to patients and their pain, sorrow, and tragedy. When a loved one has been injured, I speak to families and often tell them of my brother Eric, my mom, my dad, and my son Brian. I let them know that I understand their pain because I have been in their shoes many times before. I try to use this connection to help them make the best decisions they can for their own loved ones.

I tell patients about Eric and subtly indicate that survival is not always the best option or outcome. Sometimes letting go is a more humane decision than pushing for everything to be done. I only say this from experience. My brother would have never wanted to be what he has become. I will never forget when, a year or so after his accident, my brother Eric painstakingly but very clearly spelled out on his board, *What did I ever do to deserve this?*

With my brother, I have learned the difference between survival and quality of life. I use this life experience to try to educate families who are in the direct throes of tragedy.

I tell others about my mother and indicate that more is not always better. To think of what she went through with brain surgery, radiation, and chemotherapy—to watch her hair fall out and feel miserable day after day, only to die three short months later. We put her through hell for her last few months on this earth, and for what? I know the answer. The answer is that we did not want to accept the truth that she was going to die, and we could not let go. We didn't know any better. We wanted to do everything to try to keep our mother in our lives for as long as we could for our own selfish reasons, but somehow forgot about what was really best for our mom.

So often we put loved ones through treatment to treat ourselves—to treat our own pain. This is true of both families and the treating doctors. We so badly don't want to lose someone that we do what is right for ourselves but lose sight of what is right for the patient. It's okay not to give treatment to someone you love if it's the right thing to do for them. The hardest part of letting go is accepting the permanency of death—accepting that you will never see that person again or have them in your life once you make that final decision not to treat. I try to help families become comfortable with this idea of letting go and to help them take the burden of guilt off of their shoulders.

Then there is my dad. I knew when to let go and stop treatment. It was my father's time, and I needed to accept that and allow him to die. And I did so because I knew my dad would have wanted me to. In the end, you have to let go of your own feelings to do what is right for the person who is suffering.

I have written this chapter to show you that I am a real person just like each of you with my own set of life experiences and losses. But I also want you to know that each experience we have in life continually changes and molds who we are as individuals. It is then up to each person to use these experiences to change his or her future actions accordingly and, perhaps, for the better.

I think of my lost loved ones frequently, but nothing compares to the loss of my Brian. Losing my parents at a fairly young age was hard, but I have been able to deal with it fairly well and move on. With Brian's death, I feel much different, as if I have been pushed over an edge and can never return. I am now forced to move forward through unforgiving territory, because there is no going back. Life will always be different from this point forward, so much more so than at any other time in my past. Yet I have hope that tragedy will be used to bring about positive change. For it is through our own life experiences and lessons that we can make the world a better place for us all to live in.

Chapter 6

Turning Tragedy into Hope

The phone call we received early on the morning of Brian's accident is a phone call that every parent hopes never to receive. It is not something that you can prepare for, and certainly not something you can hide from. The days to come after Brian's death were filled with pain and anguish we had never experienced before, but we also began to feel a glimmer of hope as friends and family appeared at our doorstep to help in any way they could. I imagine that they felt a sense of helplessness and an overwhelming desire to ease the pain and suffering of others.

Now that Brian is buried and some time has passed, Cindy and I have felt the positive energy that has been bestowed upon us by our family, friends, and community. Only through the experience of our son's death have we come to realize the compassion and overwhelming sense of goodness that all people have within themselves to help transform an unfathomable tragedy into an emerging state of hope. Only in death do we realize just how many lives one individual can touch in such a short lifetime and in such a positive way! We are coming to understand that Brian's death was not in vain, because so much good and hope has been instilled in so many people he knew. As a family, we hope to bring meaning and benefit to a senseless tragedy by memorializing our son for the betterment of others.

To this end, my wife and I knew we had to capture this "energy," for lack of a better term, and turn it into something positive. We started by placing a memorial fund box at the funeral home during Brian's showings. In two days, with over 1,200 people passing through the funeral home to see Brian, we raised $8,000. As we saw the outpouring of generosity, we then researched how to set up a permanent fund. A close friend well versed in these matters helped us set up a permanent 501(c) charitable fund through the Toledo Community Foundation. Simultaneously, we had a memorial website: **www.brianmatters.com** set up for Brian with a direct link to the TCF so donations could be made online or sent by check directly to the TCF.

From there, I needed to get the word out. I contacted the *Toledo Blade* newspaper as well as Channel 13 news station to tell of Brian's story and promote the fund as well as his website. Several nice articles and TV stories were done on the tragedy of Brian's death. Lastly, I sent out more than 2,000 letters to every physician in the Toledo area and to a multitude of Toledo-area businesses to expose each of them to Brian's story. The letter described who Brian was as a person and what our goal for the donations would be.

The Brian N. Hoeflinger Memorial Fund is intended to benefit organizations, programs, and projects that reflect Brian's life passions and determination to succeed, as well as encompass his continual desire to help and comfort others. Our hope is that these grants will touch the lives of others in a positive direction, as did Brian. Our goal is to sustain the fund into perpetuity. To have the fund become self-perpetuating, we were told that a minimum of $100,000 would be needed to be raised. We had our goal.

All that I have mentioned thus far was accomplished in the first two weeks after Brian's death. For me, it gave my life purpose, as so much of my purpose in life had been taken away during those first horrible weeks without Brian.

After the website, fund, and interviews with the media were completed, I felt a sense of relief. I had completed something to bring meaning to my son's death. At that point, I returned to work as a neurosurgeon. My days were emotional and filled with an overwhelming sense of emptiness. I came home early each day, as I would begin to feel suffocated at work. I needed to come home by early afternoon to be in the house where my son once lived. Sounds strange, but it was like an intense homing signal would suddenly go off in me each day around noon, calling me back home.

As each day went on, I needed more than work to fulfill me. I needed a continuing purpose, and to bring about something positive from Brian's death. Given his love of golf, I knew a memorial golf tournament was in the future. Within a month of my son's death, I contacted an acquaintance of ours who was the director of a yearly LPGA tournament here in Toledo. He knew Brian well, as his son played golf with my son. I met with him and proposed the idea of a golf tournament in Brian's honor. I had no idea how to set up a golf tournament but knew we could do it. He liked the idea, and work on the tournament began.

I wanted to have two simultaneous tournaments on the same day, one for junior golfers and one for adults. Given Brian's close involvement in junior golf over the past four years, I knew we needed a separate tournament for all of Brian's friends, including the junior golf community, to play in his honor. I also thought it would be nice to have a common reception at the end of the day for both the adults and kids to attend together, many of whom would be parents with their children.

It had now been five weeks after Brian's death, and planning for the golf tournaments had begun. In the meantime, Brian's memorial fund was growing and had raised $40,000 thus far. People were visiting his website and reading about him. I placed the media articles on the website for people to read. We included many pictures of Brian throughout his life, college acceptance letters, and a short video of him and his brother performing Ping-Pong tricks in our house so that anyone who visited the website could get an authentic feeling for who Brian was.

As the plans for the golf tournaments unfolded, I quickly realized that we could not do it alone. We had called each golf course and secured a date of Saturday, June 1, but that was about it. So we formed a committee of volunteers and started to have meetings every two weeks. The committee was basically a group of our friends who all knew Brian and each other very well. At the first meeting, we set an outline of what needed to be accomplished, and tasks were assigned from there. From that first meeting, I could see that this was really going to happen, and "Birdies for Brian," as we named it, was born.

Over the next few weeks, we booked the reception hall, cultivated donations for food and tournament prizes, ordered T-shirts and signage for hole sponsors, scheduled volunteers to work each event, advertised and signed people up for the event, arranged payment collections, and so on. My job was to find 18 major hole sponsors for each tournament. After work each day, I called or spoke in person to as many potential sponsors as I could think of, both people I knew and people I did not. For the tournament at Sylvania Country Club, we were ultimately able to garnish 22 major sponsorships. For the junior golf tournament at Ottawa Park, I obtained sponsorships from local high schools and from many of the nursing staff at the hospitals where I work. Everything was falling into place. All we had to do was hope for good weather.

Finally the day came. All our hard work had led to this day, with a forecast of 100 percent chance of rain. I lay in bed at 4:30 a.m., listening to the thunder and pouring rain. There was no backup plan, no rain date. But the rain stopped just as the morning tournament for the kids started at 8:30, and did not resume until that evening when the afternoon tournament was completed after 6:30. Despite the 100 percent chance of rain forecast for that day, we had intermittent clouds and sunshine all day for both tournaments. The turnout was phenomenal, with 109 golfers at Ottawa Park golf course and 130 golfers at the Sylvania Country Club course, and more than 300 people at the evening reception.

The first annual Birdies for Brian tournament was an overwhelming success. We raised $40,000 from the tournament itself, and with the fund now at $71,000, we raised over $110,000 in just three months. But even more important was the fun and camaraderie that was had that day. It felt like a day of reunion for many, especially the junior golfers. I watched as many of them who hadn't seen each other in months or years, or maybe had attended school together when they were younger, gave each other hugs and handshakes on the course.

The tournament brought people together for a common purpose and reunited many. A number of Brian's friends have told us how they have reconnected with friends from the past as a result of his death. When I think about it, Brian's death has reconnected a community by bringing friends—old and new—together, as well as reconnecting families to what is truly important in life: each other. As I reflected on the day, I realized that this golf tournament had in a small way shone a positive light into the lives of others through the tragedy of Brian's death.

~~~

Around the time of the golf tournament, I also started to feel a different set of feelings regarding my son's death. Each time I thought about the night he died, I became more angry at the role that alcohol had played in his death. Brian had been drinking vodka that night, made a bad decision to drive under the influence of alcohol, and lost his life as a result. It was hard to face the fact that our son had been drinking, but that certainly was a fact that needed to be addressed. It would have been much easier to ignore and bury that particular detail surrounding Brian's death, but if we did that, then no one could learn or benefit from his mistake. Cindy and I quickly realized that we would need to talk to teenagers as well as parents about the dangers of teenage drinking, especially binge drinking. The pain we have gone through is nothing short of pure agony. If we could save just one innocent life and prevent one family from having to experience this hideous pain, it would be worth the effort.

As we thought of this new endeavor we were about to undertake, we realized that a powerful presentation would be needed to make a lasting impact on those watching and listening to our story. Thus began a new chapter in our lives. We first looked back through our family photo albums and pulled out selected pictures and video to illustrate the beautiful life we had and the wonderful times we had shared together. I needed to make people understand that Brian was a person just like them, with a lifetime of happy memories. We set this portion of the presentation to uplifting music. In addition, we showed his many accomplishments, including his grade transcripts from high school with a 4.5 GPA, an ACT score of 32, golfing accomplishments, and a college acceptance letter to UNC at Chapel Hill—all to show his commitment, hard work, and determination to succeed.

Then the music stops, there is silence, and stark pictures of walls of vodka bottles appear on the screen, prompting a hollow feeling of emptiness as you stare at the rows of transparent bottles. The slide show then transitions into an extensive array of pictures of the crash site with Brian's mangled car as the somber music begins. Suddenly, you see Brian from a distance lying in his casket, lifeless, followed by his gravestone appearing through a blanket of clouds. A final picture of his burial vault shows his birth date and the date he died. The music then transitions back to an uplifting theme, with final pictures of Brian golfing.

We created this very emotional yet graphic presentation in hopes of eliciting a lasting effect on our audience. The next portion of the talk is a slide presentation of eye-opening statistics regarding teenage drinking. The presentation closes with an inspirational talk from my wife, encouraging teenagers to take a stand against teenage drinking, after which they are invited to sign a pledge against it. With our first presentations, I think we achieved the desired effect. Our first presentation was to approximately 400 students at St. Ursula Academy, an all-girls high school. Much of the crowd was crying as the slide show progressed, and the response to our talk was overwhelming. A majority of the students came forward to sign the pledge.

We have given our presentation more than 10 times now, with the largest audience composed of 1,450 students and teachers. For the fall, we have six talks scheduled so far, including a talk at the University of Findlay in Findlay, Ohio; the Toledo Academy of Medicine; and multiple high schools and parent organizations. If you go to our website, **www.brianmatters.com**, you will find a listing of all our upcoming talks.

In concluding this chapter, I want to leave you with a final thought. I want to share a small portion of a paper that Brian had recently written for school, which he titled "Message in a Bottle." The paper was to reflect to someone else what he had learned in life thus far. The final line of his paper read,

Even the smallest of accomplishments is greatly appreciated in the eyes of a positive person because it is another step in the right direction.

We cannot always know what effect our efforts have had, but every small step matters if we are to make a difference in the lives of others. Brian believed in helping others and making an impact by example.

We hope that the tragic example of our son's death will help teenagers to realize that no real good comes from drinking alcohol. You may feel pretty cool when you are drinking, but let me tell you that it's not cool when you get raped, injured, or killed. I know you don't think anything could ever happen to you when you drink, but that is exactly what Brian used to say, and look at what drinking got him. Remember, there are no second chances when you're dead. Please think about that last statement, and think about all that Brian lost as a result of alcohol.

Chapter 7

The Sobering Statistics

As I think about Brian's death, I realize he has become another statistic. So many people are injured or killed as a result of alcohol and teenage drinking. The statistics are overwhelming. Cindy and I have begun giving presentations on teenage drinking and all of the sobering statistics associated with it. As we present the information, we try to emphasize that the data is composed of real people with real lives. An actual person like Brian who had such a wonderful life is now one of these numbers. Looking only at numbers is a dehumanizing way of looking at life outcomes. I hope that we never lose sight of the tragedy and pain in the lives of the people who make up the statistics we are about to review. With this in mind, I would like to walk you through the unbelievable data surrounding alcohol and teenage drinking.

Alcohol is the third leading cause of death in the 15- to 24-year-old age group, surpassed only by accidents and homicide. But if grouped together, alcohol-related car accidents are the number one cause of death in teenagers. Alcohol is widespread among teens. By the end of high school, nearly 80 percent of teenagers have drunk alcohol, and 37 percent have done so by eighth grade. The prevalence of alcohol in the teenage years is astounding. Underage drinkers account for 11 percent of the alcohol consumed in the US. About 9.7 million teens in the United States currently drink alcohol. That is nearly the number of people living in the entire state of Ohio. If we break it down by grade, 25 percent of eighth graders, 49 percent of tenth graders, and 62 percent of twelfth graders have been drunk. Studies show that 13,000 teens will take their first drink of alcohol each day. Focusing specifically on seniors in high school, 80 percent have drunk alcohol at some point, 74 percent have drunk in the past year, 62 percent have been drunk, and 3.6 percent use alcohol on a daily basis.

I hope that in light of these statistics, you will consider that there may be a problem in this country with teens and alcohol. Let's continue. Those who start drinking as teens are four times more likely to become alcoholics later in life. And 90 percent of alcoholics begin drinking alcohol as a teenager! Approximately one in six teenagers has experienced "blackout spells" where they could not remember the previous evening as a result of heavy alcohol use. Think of how vulnerable you become to injury, rape, and/or death when you can't even remember what you did the night before. Among college students specifically, alcohol annually contributes to 1,700 deaths, 600,000 injuries, and 97,000 cases of sexual assault. Despite these amazing statistics, teenagers never believe any of these things could happen to them. But as I said before, the numbers quoted above represent real people who also thought it could never happen to them.

Now to the topic of binge drinking, which is the most common pattern of excessive alcohol use in the United States for both adults and teenagers. By definition, binge drinking is consuming five or more drinks for men or four or more drinks for women in a one- to two-hour period. Basically, it means consuming a large amount of alcohol in a short period of time. About 90 percent of the alcohol consumed by youth under the age of 21 in the US is in the form of binge drinking. By the way, a drink is considered 1.5 ounces of hard liquor like vodka, 12 ounces of beer, or 5 ounces of wine. Given that the average person is able to metabolize alcohol at the rate of only one drink per hour, the amount of alcohol remaining in the bloodstream can add up fast.

Up to 45 percent of high school students report drinking alcohol in the past 30 days, most of whom are binge drinking, and one-third of high school seniors report at least one occasion of binge drinking in the past two weeks. A recent study which polled 16,000 high school seniors from 2005 to 2011 showed that 20 percent said they'd had five or more drinks in a row in the past two weeks, but 10 percent said they'd had 10 or more drinks at a time, and 5.6 percent said they'd had 15 or more drinks. This takes us into the realm of extreme binge drinking. The study goes on to say that drinking at this level would produce blood alcohol levels of four to five times the legal limit for an adult. Think of what could happen if a young adult or teenager was to get behind the wheel of a car with a blood alcohol level four to five times the legal limit!

Binge drinking is one of the leading preventable causes of death in this country. An average of 80,000 deaths per year are connected to binge drinking. Even one night of binge drinking can harm your liver, damage your brain, or, in a worst-case scenario, end your life. Here is a brief list of the harm alcohol can expose you to, especially at a young age: stroke; liver disease; brain damage; sexually transmitted diseases; unintended pregnancy; unintentional injuries such as car accidents, falls, and drowning; intentional injuries such as sexual assault, domestic violence, and firearm injuries; and of course death, to name a few. By drinking and becoming drunk, you place yourself at increased risk for any or all of the above. When you think about it, no true benefit comes from drinking.

Lastly, I would like to discuss the topic of drinking and driving. Car accidents are the leading cause of death for everyone ages 5 to 34, and one in three car accident deaths involves a drunk driver. Those who binge drink are 14 times more likely to drink and drive than those who do not binge drink. On average, someone dies as a result of drunk driving every 53 minutes, and someone is injured as a result of drunk driving every 90 seconds. In 2012, there were nearly 300,000 incidents of drinking and driving each day. That's more than 2 million people driving under the influence of alcohol per week! At any given moment, 1 in 50 drivers is legally intoxicated, and that number jumps to 1 in 10 on the weekends. Even at an alcohol level of .05, which represents a level obtained by approximately two drinks and is within the legal limit for adults, males are 18 times more likely and females 54 times more likely to be involved in a motor vehicle accident compared to those not drinking. These few statistics should make it clear that drinking and driving do not mix.

So why do teens drink? Possibilities include that it is a new experience for them and makes them feel more like an adult. It certainly can be viewed as fun and exciting. Many people drink because it relaxes them and they feel more sociable. Others drink to forget their problems or do so because of social pressures to fit in. My guess is that it's a combination of many of these factors. What teens do not fully understand is that alcohol is a depressant that slows down the brain and body. Sure, at first you feel happy, more sociable, and good about yourself. But this quickly changes with each additional drink.

The first abilities that are altered are judgment and coordination. An impaired driver cannot recognize a potentially dangerous situation and react quickly enough to avoid an accident. Unfortunately, because judgment is impaired, drivers under the influence of alcohol do not realize they have had too much to drink. Do you realize that after drinking a six-pack of beer or six shots of alcohol, your chances of being in a drunk driving accident rise to 44 percent?

Unfortunately, many teens don't think there is anything wrong with drinking. They view it as an acceptable activity. And since they don't drink every night, they don't see the potential harm in it. They mistakenly believe that "bad things can't happen to me because I'm young and invincible." But if we remember my son Brian for a moment, we know that this is not true. He was not invincible, and it did happen to him. It can certainly happen to you!

So let me ask you, why would you keep doing it? How do we make you understand that you can have fun without using alcohol?

We hope that with education about the statistics like those above, teens will start to reconsider their need to drink alcohol. Our family is now living in the haunting shadow of these all-too-real statistics. Brian is gone, and there is no way of getting him back. I hope you will heed this warning and realize it could all too easily be you. Brian has no second chance to redo things or learn from his mistake. But you do have the chance to learn from Brian's mistake and say no to alcohol. Remember, using alcohol is a choice, and only you can say no to that choice. Please choose wisely!

Chapter 8

The Investigation: Who's Accountable?

Yesterday was the Fourth of July. Cindy asked me if I wanted to play golf, which she rarely does, and I said sure. This was the first time we've played together since Brian's death. It was a hot, overcast day with little breeze. We talked very little the first three holes, and there was an uncomfortable feeling about the situation. We were sitting alone in our cart on hole #4 in the middle of this beautiful tree-lined fairway. No other golfers were in sight. The air was still.

Cindy turned to me and said, "It's too quiet out here today." She started to cry. "Brian should be here."

"I know," I said, and started to tear up. Nothing feels the same since Brian died. It has been five months since his death, and the overwhelming feeling of loss is still strong.

"Right when I think I'm doing better," she said, "the feeling of Brian being dead overwhelms me."

I feel the same. The hurt that we feel is like nothing we have experienced in our lives. It doesn't let up for any length of time. I continue to live from day to day with nothing to look forward to. I feel no real happiness or joy.

Cindy and I began to talk about why it happened and what we could have done to stop it. We have no real answers. As time has passed, we have started to feel angry—an emotion that most parents would surely experience when they lose a child unexpectedly. Anger at ourselves for not protecting Brian and preventing his death. Anger at the liquor store that sold the alcohol. Anger at Brian for drinking, acting irresponsibly, and driving under the influence of alcohol. And anger at the hosting residence where Brian was drinking.

When I think about all of this, I wonder who, if anyone, should be held accountable for Brian's death. In this chapter I'll review the possible contributing factors leading to his death, without holding judgment against any particular party.

So who, if anyone, should bear responsibility? Is it the liquor store that sold these minors vodka, or the parents who did not supervise the kids in their basement, or us as Brian's parents for not knowing he was drinking alcohol? Or is it all Brian's fault for drinking and driving under the influence? What about the kids at the party who knew Brian was drunk and yet let him leave the party drunk in his car? Should they bear any responsibility? Or is it ultimately our society, which is not doing enough about all of the above?

Let's review the facts.

First, we know the boys bought the alcohol at a state liquor store without showing their IDs. How did this happen? It is against the law to sell alcohol to minors under the age of 21, and it is the law to check IDs if the person looks under 40 years of age. Yet my young-looking 18-year-old son and his two underage friends walked into a state liquor store and were able to buy a 1.75-liter bottle of vodka without being carded. It's clear that the liquor store broke the law. In addition, the two boys who were with Brian that night have told state investigators that they drank primarily out of the bottle of vodka they had bought at the liquor store—the same bottle of vodka that led to Brian becoming drunk. What should happen to the store, the owner, and the clerk who sold the alcohol to them? Through a state investigation, the store clerk has been charged and is awaiting trial. The liquor store has lost its license to sell hard liquor but can still sell beer and wine.

Regarding any civil proceedings, private counsel has indicated that no successful case could be brought against the liquor store or store clerk as it pertains to Brian's death because of the way the laws are written. According to Ohio law, a liquor permit holder can be found liable when the permit holder sells intoxicating beverages to an underage person and that intoxicated underage person causes an injury to an innocent third party. However, Ohio law holds that there is no valid claim against a liquor permit holder by an underage person for self-inflicted injury or death due to being intoxicated. Thus the law differentiates between injury to a minor (defined as someone under the age of 21) by their own doing as a result of intoxication versus injury to a third party caused by an intoxicated minor. The laws seem to hold the intoxicated minor alone responsible for his or her actions regardless of who provided the alcohol which resulted in their intoxication. The law views the minor as an adult for all intents and purposes, and thus concludes that the young adult drinks the alcohol voluntarily against the law and cannot hold others responsible for his or her own actions while intoxicated.

With this in mind, it makes one wonder why it is illegal to sell or provide alcohol to minors in the first place. For what purpose was this law created? One would assume the law was written to prevent minors from gaining access to alcohol and drinking. The legal age for drinking is 21, and therefore, the law suggests that minors less than 21 years of age are not able to make proper decisions when it comes to alcohol. So why would the law seem to protect a limited class of individuals, that being the innocent third-party victims, but not protect the minor who has gained access to alcohol but is underage and not able to make appropriate decisions regarding alcohol? The two lines of thought are contradictory, meaning minors under the age of 21 by law cannot legally buy or drink alcohol, presumably because they are not mature enough to handle the alcohol responsibly, but the law also states that if minors under the age of 21 do gain access to alcohol and become intoxicated, then they are viewed as adults and they alone are fully responsible for their actions thereafter. The law would like to have it both ways, but the law would seem discriminatory against the intoxicated minor.

If we want to block minors' access to alcohol, then stiffer laws and punishment need to be implemented to send a stronger message to the store owners, their employees, and other providers of alcohol that this behavior will not be tolerated. Intoxicated youth should be held accountable and punished when caught consuming alcohol, but the provider should share equally in this punishment and should be held liable for any injury which occurs to the minor as a result of his or her intoxication. I would propose this as a new law or extension of current law. Obviously, this is only one step along the path toward stopping teenage drinking, but it's a big step in the right direction.

Then there are the parents who host drinking parties for teenagers.

In the specific case of my son, the parents involved had no knowledge that the kids were drinking in their basement. But for discussion purposes, should parents, in general, bear no responsibility for events and actions that occur in their home? If parents can simply deny that they have knowledge of what is going on in their own home, how can we ever hold anybody accountable for their actions, or in this case inactions? Nothing will ever change with this type of mentality in place, because there is no fear of consequences. If we are to change things regarding hosting laws, we have to give hosting parents something to be concerned about.

Is it enough to plead ignorance and say you didn't know? The actual law in Ohio, called the "social host law," states that no person who is the owner or occupant of any public or private place shall knowingly allow any underage person to remain in or on the premises while possessing or consuming beer or intoxicating liquor, unless the alcohol is provided to that underage person by a parent (or by someone else as long as that underage person's parent is present). The key is that you cannot *knowingly* provide alcohol to a minor if that minor is not your child and/or the minor's parent is not present. If you say you didn't know, then you are released of all responsibility.

In addition, to take it a step further, Ohio law supports that social hosts who do actually provide intoxicating beverages to an underage adult are not liable or held responsible when that underage adult drives a car and fatally injures him- or herself. Again, the law views the intoxicated minor as an adult who alone is responsible for his or her own actions, despite gaining access to the alcohol by a host. The hosting law needs to be changed or modified appropriately to protect the minor as well as the innocent third party.

Let's look at the facts: the night my son died, Brian, who is a minor, drank alcohol with other minors in a homeowners basement while the homeowners themselves were present in the house and had knowledge that there was a gathering of minors in their basement. They did not know the kids were drinking alcohol. The next logical question would then be, what responsibility should any homeowner bear for events that happen in their own house when they are indeed home and present in that house? This question needs to be readdressed by the law. It seems to me that the current law protects the parents and not the minor. In that context, pleading ignorance is a valid excuse. Obviously, no one can prove that the alcohol caused the car accident that killed Brian, but it would be hard to believe that the alcohol was not a contributing factor. The bottom line is, who is responsible for the alcohol the minor was drinking?

A big problem with society today is that no one wants to take responsibility for their actions. As parents, should we not be somewhat responsible for what happens in our own homes when our children are involved? If we really want to get serious about teenage drinking and parents hosting parties for our children, then there has to be zero tolerance for this type of activity, and parents have to be held accountable for what goes on in their own homes.

Next, there are the kids who were with Brian at the party. Do they bear any responsibility? Perhaps not, other than the moral obligation to try and stop a friend from drinking and driving, which they did.

What about us, Brian's parents? Did we fail him? We have been sent several anonymous letters stating so. Did we not raise him properly and teach him not to drink, and especially not to drink and drive? We thought we did, but obviously we were wrong. We certainly are going to try even harder with our remaining three children, but that will not help Brian. And what of our punishment? I think we all know the answer to that question.

That leaves Brian. He was 18 and should have known better. He should have known not to buy alcohol from a state liquor store that sells to minors and, in the case of my son, did not check ID's. He should have known better to not drink the alcohol at an unsupervised party. He should have known to listen to his parents, who spoke to him many times about alcohol and the dangers of drinking and driving. And lastly, he should have known better than to walk out of a house drunk. But he didn't know better on all counts. Should all the responsibility for his death then lie on him? The law would say "yes."

What of the role of the alcohol? Is the alcohol to blame for any part of this? We certainly know that alcohol clouds the decision-making process, and if someone is drunk, the alcohol—not the person—is making the majority of the decisions at that point. He is certainly the one who helped buy the alcohol, drink it, and drive under the influence, but the alcohol was the driving force of his bad decisions that night once he took the first drink. His mistake was taking that first drink, and he was punished severely for that mistake. So far, he is the only one who has been punished or made to take any responsibility for his death.

And if we assume that alcohol played a role in his death, should those who provided access to the alcohol not bear some responsibility for his death? Thus far, the store clerk has been charged with a first-degree misdemeanor for selling alcohol to a minor. This wasn't the first time he'd done it. Five months earlier, he had been fined $150 for the same offense. The liquor store has lost its license to sell hard liquor permanently. But the store clerk, liquor store, and the parents who hosted the party will have no charges brought against them pertaining to Brian's death, as Ohio law does not view any of the above parties to be responsible for Brian's death. Many of the kids at the party may feel guilty about Brian's death and will bear this burden for years to come, but their lives have gone on.

~~~

Cindy and I have started to give talks to both teens and adults regarding teenage drinking and the dangers of alcohol, with the hope of bringing about positive change as a result of this tragedy. In our presentations, we talk about the dangers of hosting an unsupervised party and advocate at least checking on the kids once in a while to make sure they are not drinking in the house.

As I think over all that has happened, I believe it is our society that ultimately needs to change the most. We need to have stricter laws and punishment for those who facilitate teenage drinking. We can never win this battle if we continue to tolerate this behavior. Stricter laws should not be viewed as a punishment but as an opportunity or "second chance" to do the right thing and save lives in the future. As I said before, I only wish Brian had been caught drinking or arrested that night. Yes, his reputation would have been tarnished, but he would still be alive, and he would have learned a valuable lesson. He paid the ultimate price for his mistake.

Many in our society would view my son's death as his responsibility alone because no one forced him to drink that night. The choice was his alone. Or was it? Does our society bear any of the responsibility for making alcohol too accessible to teens and for shaping their perception of alcohol? What of the manner in which alcohol is made available to teens and is advertised in a glamorous fashion on TV and on billboards? Are they made to think drinking is fun and cool when they see sexy advertisements promoting alcohol at sophisticated parties, or a televised commercial during the PGA golf championship glamorously advertising Belvedere vodka, the same vodka my son drank the night he died? Could it be that our society is influencing our youth to drink alcohol, while at the same time granting access to it before they reach the age of 21?

We should all take a good look at ourselves before we place blame and responsibility on any one individual or group. Is it not our job as parents and as a society to take the choice of drinking alcohol away from our children, at least until they reach the age of 21? It is the law! When did teenage drinking become the norm? And why is it so readily accepted by so many in our society today? We all have the opportunity to play a role in changing things if we make the effort. Sitting back and doing nothing accomplishes just that: ***nothing***. For our children's sake, we must get involved.

~~~

As Cindy and I finished our round of golf that day, we realized that no amount of anger or blame will bring Brian back. It is natural for people to want to blame others for their problems and misfortune. I have learned this well during my career as a neurosurgeon. I know that sometimes bad things happen to good people for unknown reasons, and there isn't necessarily someone to blame for it or any way to stop it. On the other hand, there are often steps that can be taken to change things for the betterment of others. It is our hope that the contents of this chapter will promote discussion of these matters and encourage people to become proactive against teenage drinking for the good of generations to come. We need to get involved now if we are to change things for our future, and particularly for our children's future.

Chapter 9

Who Was Brian Hoeflinger the Person?

By this point, I imagine many of you are wondering just who was this kid named Brian Hoeflinger, and is there more to hear about him as a person? In this chapter, I would like to give you the opportunity to read some of his actual writings verbatim and the thoughts shared about him by his friends after his death. In doing so, I think you will gain an even better appreciation for the special person Brian Nicholas Hoeflinger was.

Message in a Bottle

I carefully rolled the piece of paper with a smile of satisfaction on my face. I pushed it through the narrow neck of the bottle and then sealed it with a cork. I hurled the bottle as far as I could off the pier, hoping that it would not wash back up onto the shore. I wondered who would find my bottle, and if they would read my message, which brought me back to what I had written:

To whoever may find this letter, I first want to congratulate you for taking the initiative to remove the cork and read it. I have written this letter as a way to communicate what I have learned in my life so far. There is a fine line between being positive and being negative. A positive person seizes opportunities and takes everything a situation has to offer. On the contrary, a negative person cringes at opportunity and does what he can to always see the negative aspects of a situation. Thus, I have realized that always keeping a positive outlook in any situation, especially in the midst of adversity, yields much more beneficial results than negativity at any level.

"The one who thinks he can is right, yet the one who thinks he cannot is also right." Simply, both positive and negative people can achieve exactly what they want to achieve. However, it stems back to which outlook they have on life. A person with a positive outlook wants to achieve goals that are above and beyond; his aspirations will not be easy to attain, but he will do whatever it takes to attain them. He is positive in all situations and pounces on opportunity because it is only through opportunity that one can move forward. Likewise, a negative person is also right. He believes that anything beyond his reach cannot be achieved. He fears success, and for this reason, he will not seize opportunities. He is forever trapped within the bounds of his own negativity, a cage that is difficult to escape. Though it is easier to see the world through a negative lens, a positive outlook can take a person far beyond his original intentions.

Most successful people see the glass half full and take

advantage of all situations. By having such a positive outlook, they achieve what at first might appear to be impossible. I'm not saying that a negative person is worse than a positive person; after all, everyone is negative at times. A positive person, however, will enjoy all aspects of life much more than a negative person, simply because of the outlook he has on life. And therefore, with a positive mindset, a person sees his achievements on a much higher pedestal. Even the smallest of accomplishments is greatly appreciated in the eyes of a positive person because it is another step in the right direction.

After reliving my message, I smiled and began walking down the pier toward the beach.

Growing Closer to Christ Through Service

Service. One word defines the mission of the Christian faith. It is through service that we not only become closer to Christ, but we also strengthen our relationship with the people around us.

For twelve years I was enrolled in a Christian institution. However, this has marked the first year of which my education has not been affiliated with religion. I attended a Catholic grade school from kindergarten through eighth grade, and then moved onto a Jesuit high school until my junior year. I chose to transfer to a public school for my senior year, knowing that it would have no effect on my faith life. I believe that faith is an important part of every person's life, but going to church can only take us so far on our journeys. It is through dedicated service to your community and strong morals for the people you serve that you can truly fulfill the mission of the Christian faith.

I have volunteered at several organizations throughout my life, but especially during my high school career. One experience, though, sticks out to me more than all the rest. During my junior year, I was involved in a program in which I tutored inner city children. I have a lot to offer as a tutor because I have the ability to work with people on their level and logically instruct them. I helped first graders improve their reading skills, and also tutored seventh and eighth graders in math and science. Over my four months working with students, I could see obvious improvement in their skills, but more importantly in their attitude toward school. The satisfaction received from an experience like this is priceless, as there is no greater reward than that of serving others. Seeing the smiles of the children every week and knowing that they are expecting to see your face makes you feel especially good about yourself. The true service I gave to these children was not their academic improvement or the friendships I created with them; what I accomplished went far beyond that. The fact that they appreciate school more and can understand how beneficial education can be is the greatest service I could give to the children.

Service is truly about giving up part of yourself for the betterment of others, and the others do not necessarily have to be less fortunate than you. To me, simply helping a friend or being kind to a stranger is service in itself. By doing things like these, you are strengthening your understanding of what Christianity is all about: you are moving closer to Christ.

Confidence Is the Key

After reflecting on the events of my life, I am brought back to the day of July 1st, 2011. It was on this Friday afternoon that I won my first golf tournament. I began playing golf in the summer of seventh grade, and I immediately fell in love with the sport. I practiced every day and had a keen focus on improving. Three years later, my hard work and diligence paid off. I was competing in the Toledo District Match Play Championship, and I barely made the field after a poor qualifying round. I was competing against several players who were much better than me, and I had little expectations for myself. My goal was to make it as far as I could in the match play rounds, whether that be elimination in the first round or elimination in the final round. In my first round match, I was paired against a fellow teammate from my high school golf team. I realized during this round that I was actually playing the best golf of my life. I advanced and made it to the semi-finals. The semi-final round was probably the most scary round of my entire life, considering I was paired against one of the golfers who had gone to states the previous year (and I was not even a varsity golfer that year). After 18 holes, we were tied, so we moved onto the first playoff hole. It was the first playoff of my career, and I was extremely nervous. I hit a terrible shot off the tee, but regained focus on my way to the second shot. I was able to birdie the hole and win the playoff. I distinctly remember calling my mom and telling her about my victory, as if I had already won the entire tournament. However, I was quickly knocked back to reality: I was facing one of the best golfers in the area in the final match. At this point, I was trying to win. I knew he was a better golfer, but I was determined to beat him. We were tied after 18 holes, and once again I won the first playoff hole. The relief I experienced after it was all over was incredible. I could not believe what I had just done; I had won my first tournament! I called my parents, ecstatic about my performance.

Looking back on this day, almost a year later, I realize how successful I was. This win boosted my confidence and really enabled me to play at my full potential. I considered myself a great golfer, and was a contender in every tournament after my first win. I will never forget that sunny Friday afternoon, which has drastically changed my mindset and taught me to be more confident. Confidence is the key in all aspects in life, and can unlock endless opportunities for the future.

Positive Direction Essay

Last year during Positive Direction Week, a man came to our school with Dr. Brickman. He came to talk about the dangers of alcohol. He had been in a car crash because he drove a car after drinking alcohol. He was in a coma for a while and almost died. He had to admit his mistakes in front of all of us, which was probably embarrassing. He talked about a horrible thing in his past. Since driving while drunk is illegal, he had to do various community services as a consequence. I think it would be humiliating to talk about a bad experience in your life. In his case, I think he has turned this bad experience into a positive inspiration and influence for others. He definitely had an impact on me, and I believe many others were also impacted by his words. This man is one reason I will never drive while drunk. His past experience shows how dangerous alcohol can be and has influenced me and others not to drive after having had alcohol. I think he had to be brave to go in front of an audience and talk about something he did wrong years ago. He has used this experience to educate others about the dangers of alcohol. He is making a positive change in some people, teaching them not to drive after drinking alcohol. I can use qualities like his to change my world. If I see something I don't like in my world, all I have to do is try to change it. Once I put forth an effort to change it, I have already started to make a positive change. So, when I see something that is wrong, all I have to do is try to change it positively and I am already making the world just a little bit better.

Goals

Striving to achieve a goal is a part of everyone's life at some point. Goals are not easily attained, however, and some are more difficult to reach than others. I have come to realize that all goals are indeed attainable, but not all goals are easy to achieve. Hard work and precious time is required to reach what at first might appear to be the sky. The most important thing to understand when referring to achieving a goal is that it will not happen overnight; a goal requires so much more than that.

In June of 2007, the summer between my seventh and eighth grade year, I swung a golf club for the first time. From that point forward, I dreamed of playing golf in high school, which as an eighth grader seemed close to impossible. I practiced all the time and devoted much of my energy to the game of golf. The following year, I tried out for the high school golf team. After the third day of tryouts, I received a call from the coach saying I had made the team.

However, making the team was just the beginning of my story with the game of golf. In April of 2012, I signed up to qualify for an international tournament. The following month I made it through the first round of qualifying. On June 17th, the second qualifying round would be held. The top 20 individuals would qualify to play in the Optimist International Junior Championship tournament in Florida. Every day I practiced with the goal of making it to Florida. At night, I dreamed about playing in the tournament. I spent an entire month focused on my goal to play in Florida.

After numerous days of practice and countless hours of lost sleep, I arrived in Canton, Ohio, to qualify for the Optimist tournament. It was projected that I would have to shoot no worse than five over par to qualify for Florida. I started the day with three consecutive bogeys, and was suddenly three over par after just three holes. There was not a worse feeling in the world than to see your dream, the goal you have worked so hard to attain, quickly fading away. It was at that moment I realized I had one chance; this was my one shot to achieve this one particular goal. I finished the round five over, and eventually went on to qualify in a seven-man playoff.

I have come to understand that it is by setting goals that I control my future. With this 499-word essay, I have completed the final step toward achieving a lifelong goal. Goals are an important part of everyone's lives. They allow us as humans to continue pushing forward, breaking new barriers and making new discoveries. Goals allow us to truly desire something. We can ask ourselves: How bad do I really want it? That is a question that the greatest thinkers have already answered, and it is a question that we, too, must answer in order to create our own future.

Putting for the Cure

Having played high school golf for three years, I wanted to make my final year special. Our team colors are green, black and white, but we did not like our white polos. My teammate and I jokingly talked about ordering new team shirts that were pink. I decided this was a great idea, and I took the initiative. After receiving the shipment, I took the polos to get embroidered with a special logo that would match the shirts. Once everything was completed, I took the shirts to practice and handed them out. Everyone loved the shirts, but inside it sparked an idea.

I went to my teammate and suggested the idea; he thought it was brilliant. Next, I talked to my coach, who was entirely supportive. My idea involved the pink shirts, which would be perfect since everyone on the team had one. Our team could host a fundraising event called "Putting for the Cure" where we wear our pink shirts for breast cancer awareness. The fundraiser would be held at a putt-putt course where people could donate money to our fund. All said and done, our golf team could donate the money we raised to breast cancer awareness and then wear our shirts in honor of those effected by breast cancer.

Reflection Paper

To begin, I chose to work at the soup kitchen because my dad's friend has been going there for some time. It was easy for me to just go with him to the soup kitchen, instead of my parents driving me. God Works Family Soup Kitchen is in Monroe, Michigan, so it's about a 30-minute drive. Before I went to the soup kitchen, I thought I would be serving soup to people. I thought it would be "prison style," like you see in movies. My few fears were that I didn't know anyone there, and I didn't know what to do. After the first time, though, I started to understand how things worked. When I first volunteered, I was blown away by how different it was than how I thought it would be.

God Works serves food every night at 6:00 p.m. Each night the food is made at a different church. I went on Tuesdays, so it was always at the same church. The work itself was not very hard. After I got there, around 4:45 p.m., I would help set up chairs in the gym where the food was served. The doors open at 5:30 p.m., and I would help serve coffee. After I was done with the coffee it was about 5:45 p.m., and I would wait until 6:00 p.m. At 6:00 p.m., the meals would start being served. In the kitchen, the meals would be put onto a plate, and then taken into the gym on a cart. I would help take the food out on the carts, and then put it on the serving table. After everyone had gotten their food, seconds were served. At this point, I would talk to people or eat some food myself. Then around 7:00 p.m., it was time for the people to leave and cleanup began. All the chairs had to be put away, and the table had to be folded and put away also. After cleanup, it was time to go. The low points in this experience were definitely when I had to sit and do nothing. I would rather be doing work because that is what I had come to do. The high points were times when I was working, particularly when I was pouring drinks. I was pretty good at that. I really didn't have a supervisor. I could just ask any of the other adults what I could do and they would tell me. If I had to call someone my supervisor, it would be Mr. Graham, the person I was coming with. All the volunteers were really nice, and I was able to work with them all very well. Finally, I contributed my time to help serve people who didn't have money to buy their own dinner. By giving my time, I was able to give back and help others in need.

The main sacrifice I made was just spending three and a half hours of my Tuesday afternoon away from home. This is time I would have been doing homework, but instead I went and did service work. I talked to some of the people. A lot of them had mental problems and they didn't make sense, but they were still all very nice people. I learned that I can actually help others by just doing a minor act of service. The people I served always said thank you and were very thankful for my efforts. They would often ask if they could have something just out of respect. Finally, I have decided I am going to the church with Mr. Graham on the Tuesdays that he goes. I really enjoy working there because it makes me feel good that I am helping others.

The New Testament passage from Matthew 7:21 represents my attitude toward service. "Not everyone who says to me, 'Lord, Lord,' will enter the kingdom of heaven, but only the one who does the will of my Father in Heaven." *I chose this passage because it is saying you will go to heaven if you work for the good of others on Earth. I am following this passage by serving others in the soup kitchen. This is*

God's will; to help others who are less fortunate than you. You can't just believe in God, you must serve others with the many talents God has given you.

It's All in the Mindset

I hurled the bottle into the ocean, pondering where it would wash up and who would receive my message. I smiled with a sense of satisfaction as I remembered what I had written.

The one who thinks he can is right, yet the one who thinks he cannot is also right. Simply, both positive and negative energy exist in the world. Those who think positively thirst for opportunity because through opportunity one can move forward. They realize that with their mind they can control their lives. However, with positive energy, there also exists negative energy. Those who think negatively do not realize the power of their mind. Negative thinking leaves a person trapped within the bounds of negativity, which is very hard to escape. By thinking negatively, one will never reach his full potential because he is not allowing himself to fully harness the power of his own mind.

These two modes of thinking can both lead to great things. However, negativity leads to less satisfaction and less trust. A prime example of negativity in our world can be seen in politics. Look at America, where no one has trust in the government. The president is looked at through a negative lens because people are never satisfied. All presidents make changes—some good and some bad—in the government; however, citizens often focus solely on all of the things he fails to achieve in office. Negativity pervades American society in a sense.

In addition, the concept of positive energy creating positive outcomes is widely accepted in athletics. Athletes train their minds daily in order to reach their full athletic potential. By thinking positively, they unlock a whole new realm in which they can succeed. They understand the power of their minds, and trust fully in themselves. And they realize that it is only possible to achieve their goals by first gaining full control over their minds.

Essentially, a person's mindset determines how much they will enjoy the beauty of life. Positive energy almost always renders positive results simply because of the way a situation is viewed. Failure to one who thinks positively will be viewed as a stepping-stone on the path of life. Without failing, you never learn from your mistakes. Positive people realize that failure is an essential part of life. On the contrary, failure could have detrimental effects for one who thinks negatively. He might think he is not good enough, and therefore never try to succeed again because he fears failure. The difference between positive and negative energy lies in the eye of the beholder.

Maybe my message will create an Olympic athlete. Maybe it will influence someone to become a great doctor or psychiatrist. Maybe it will have an impact on a girl, making her a wonderful, positive wife someday. Hopefully though, my message will make someone realize that the mind is the most powerful weapon one can wield.

Teeth

Society recommends that you brush your teeth at least twice a day. But why do we love our teeth so much? Teeth are vital structures in the digestive system of the body; they allow us to eat food, one of the basic necessities of life. But beyond that, our teeth allow us to express ourselves. When you meet someone, you often notice his or her smile right away. In other words, teeth add or subtract from someone's first impression of you.

First impressions are a very crucial part of our lives. As a matter of fact, a good first impression could make the difference between getting the job and being denied the position. Celebrities mesh right into the concept of first impressions. They are often viewed as symbols of beauty and perfection. With appearance always in mind, celebrities' lives essentially revolve around first impressions. Hair, eyes, clothing, and smile all build up appearance. Have you ever noticed how almost all celebrities you see in magazines have perfect smiles? This is no coincidence; the smile is recognized as a very important component of a person's beauty. People are very quick to criticize a celebrity who does not have beautiful teeth. Everyone forms opinions and makes judgments; therefore, a dentist can do wonders for a person.

Growing up, I never feared the dentist or the orthodontist; I was comfortable in that environment and was actually there quite often. My teeth were not the straightest or the whitest, but that is what is beautiful about teeth: options are available for those who were not blessed with a perfect smile. Dentists can fix cavities, making them essentially disappear. And orthodontists can install braces to completely reconfigure a smile.

Both dentists and orthodontists have a power far beyond just fixing teeth. For some time now, this power has intrigued me. The thought of being a dentist—having the ability to alter how others look at someone—fascinates me. The mechanical fixing of teeth, such as installing braces or filling a cavity, does change how others look at someone. However, the true power of a dentist or orthodontist lies in his ability to help someone far beyond just aesthetic appearance. A new, whiter, and straighter smile gives a person newfound confidence and trust in himself. This confidence of wearing a new and beautiful smile will make a difference in the aspect of first impressions.

Teeth make up every smile, which in turn impacts someone's first impression of you. A simple smile can make a huge difference in how others look at you. A smile has the power to grab attention right away because smiles are unique and beautiful. So smile big. You never get a second chance to make a first impression.

Taking a Risk

It is now late fall, and I've been attending Ottawa Hills for only three short months. To me, though, it seems like I've been there all of high school.

I took a risk last summer, and I'm very proud of that risk. I transferred from St. John's to Ottawa Hills High School for my senior year. I saw this as an opportunity to grow as an individual and transition into college.

At St. John's, I had a close circle of friends whom I had gone to grade school with, and I am still good friends with all of them. However, the new friendships I formed as a freshman at St. John's have since faded. As the years went by, most of the guys I hung out with began making decisions that I did not agree with. My friendships with them slowly disintegrated, and I started to spend more and more time with my close, small circle of friends.

I met some of the students from Ottawa Hills during April of my junior year. The students at Ottawa Hills seemed to mirror my interests more closely than the students at St. John's. I shadowed Ottawa Hills in May, and I was intrigued by both the school and the community. I realized that at Ottawa Hills, I could be in AP and honor classes as well as sports and the play. The environment was entirely different and very unique.

Shortly after I shadowed, I was pretty certain I wanted to transfer, but the voice in the back of my head was cautious. I pondered the outcomes of staying at St. John's and of transferring to Ottawa Hills. Both schools have exceptional academics, so I focused solely on the social aspects of the two schools. I realized that Ottawa Hills posed an opportunity to meet new people even though it was risky. After much consideration, I decided in the summer that I would transfer to Ottawa Hills.

I trusted my decision and always kept an optimistic outlook. I control my own destiny, and I told myself I was going to create a new positive reality. The first day of school came quickly, and I still remember that day vividly. I knew some of the faces, but I was not friends with anyone. It was very uncomfortable for the first few weeks, but I realized that people grow the most when they are out of their comfort zones, and I took it as a challenge to grow. Since those first weeks, I have formed numerous new friendships. My decision was a successful one. To this day though, I am not entirely quite sure why I transferred; back in April something just told me it was time for a change. I compared this change to a mini college transition. I was nervous but also excited that I had control to write my own future. I am now an Ottawa Hills student and will soon be graduating, after which I will be off to college to begin my new life. I cannot say how proud I am that I took the risk to transfer schools. Most seniors in high school would not be able to transfer to a new school and integrate themselves into an entirely new environment. Through this experience, I have gained confidence in myself and have grown as an individual, and I am so proud to say that I was able to accomplish all of this by taking the risk I did.

My Dream

My patient was smiling with teeth white as pearls. After two years, I removed her braces, and her teeth looked beautiful. This was the first set of braces that I had removed as an orthodontist, and I was looking forward to many more in the future. My dream had come true; I had completed my education and become an orthodontist.

All my life, my aspirations for the future have constantly been changing. Recently, however, I have decided that my dream is to become an orthodontist. Ever since I was little, I have always wanted to help people in some way, whether it be as a doctor, policeman, or dentist—I did not care. As I have grown older, though, I have put forth more thought into what I want to become.

My father is a neurosurgeon, and my mother was a pathologist. Being influenced by two doctors my entire life, I have always seen myself working in the field of medicine. I have grown up seeing the stress that my father goes through every day. He wakes up extremely early and comes home well after dinner. I do not see him some days because of how busy he is. For this reason, I have removed neurosurgery from my future job possibilities list!

I constantly thought about what I wanted to be when I grew up. I wanted to hold a position where I could help people without having to be on call every third night. I wanted a job that was not easily attained, a job that I had to work hard for. Ever since I started getting grades on my report card, I have always strived for the best grade because my mom always told me that is what I would need to become a doctor. Though my transcript from elementary school has little effect on college for me, my mom did instill hard work and effort in me.

Nothing comes easy in life, and I understand to reach the top, you must work. Becoming an orthodontist is not an easy accomplishment. It will require four years of college, four years of dentistry school, and then two more years of school to become a certified orthodontist. Many people do not want to spend that much time in school, but I realize that is what it takes to make my dream into a reality.

There have been other people who have shaped me into who I am, but really, my parents have played the largest role. I want to follow in their footsteps and become successful by my own doing. I want to someday be respected by my community not only as an orthodontist, but also as a kind and amiable person.

~~~

As you can see, Brian had a lot of good ideas and wisdom beyond his years. He was somewhat of an "old soul" for his young age.

After Brian died, teachers at school asked those who knew him to write down their memories of Brian or what he meant to them. These notes were given to me and Cindy, and I've included some of them below, along with a few notes from Facebook pages. Just as his writings help to define him as an individual, these comments from Brian's friends will help to exemplify how he was defined and viewed by others.

You will note many of the same traits being recognized over and over by friends who knew him. This common set of qualities which others are quick to note are at the essence of Brian's being—a testament to the caring, giving, positive person he truly was.

~~~

So Brian, today's been a tough day. There's a part missing in everybody at school, not only students, but the teachers as well. The entire atmosphere was different. Especially in English, we talked about you for the entire period. You happened to be the one that brought so much fun to the class. Seriously, who can forget the days when Mrs. Schoenberger would yell at you for either chatting or falling asleep? And who can forget your amazing clapping abilities? Oh yeah, Grace Wipfli brought a rose and put it behind the desk where you used to sit. It was so pretty. And Tristan shared his childhood stories about you. We cried and laughed together. How everyone behaved and supported each other throughout the day was absolutely incredible. Yes, you're THAT IMPORTANT to our community. I wish you could see all of this. I'm sure you would be glad to know how much we all cared about you. You will live on through our memories.

~~~

I am going to miss you. I am going to miss your laugh, your smile, but most of all I am just going to miss you. You were a great friend and I will never forget the times we had.

~~~

Brian, I want you to know I always thought you were probably the nicest person I've ever met. The pursuit of happiness remix came on my radio yesterday, and I thought of you and how much you loved it. I'll miss you. You'll always hold a special place in my heart.

~~~

Brian Nicholas Hoeflinger. I don't know where to begin. Ever since you were a kid, you were always going above and beyond your expectations. You were responsible and very, very smart. You were the oldest sibling, and you were our leader. I can't emphasize enough how great of a brother you are. You are hilarious and always make me laugh. You are the kindest person. I am so proud of you for making friends so easily after switching schools your senior year. You have always supported me. You made me feel important and special. You cared for others and were a great listener. Mom told me about how you cared so much for others. You hated when guys used girls. You thought it was horrible, and you treated people the right way. I always thought you were so cool. You were super strong, and I always wanted to feel your muscles. You had a 4.6 GPA. You made friends so easily, and that helped me a lot because I am shy. You were going to become an orthodontist and go to UNC. I can't believe that you never got the chance to do this. You were going to have kids, and I was too, and our children would play together at Thanksgiving. You had so much to offer. I still can't believe this has happened. You are the brightest kid I know. You were the best brother ever, and I couldn't have asked for a better one. You have impacted many people, and we all love you. Rest in Peace, Brian.

~~~

Every time I saw Brian in the halls, he ALWAYS had a smile on his face. When I saw him smiling, it made me smile too. He will be in our thoughts forever. Ottawa Hills will always miss him and love him.

~~~

Every day you lit up every room you walked into. I love your laugh and your amazing outlook on life. I'll never forget our weekly team questionnaires in English. I'll remember you and your contagious smile forever.

~~~

I love you, and I promise to live a good life for you. I will show you how much I miss you through my actions, not my words. I will put God above everything, just as you did. I will treat others the way you would have treated them—with love and compassion. I will do as you did, and make everyone around me smile and laugh. I will strive to grow myself like you did—spiritually, physically, and mentally. I will do all of these things on a daily basis in honor of you and your beautiful legacy. Your honor will supersede words and thoughts. It will take physical form and manifest itself through my hands and feet. I will continue doing your work. I promise. Love you, BNH.

~~~

The amount a person can affect the people around them is incredible. I always saw Brian supporting his brother at games and cheering on his friends. He projected a light that will never be put out. His faith and positive energy will never be forgotten. Brian would say,

"I just hope when all is said and done that my elevator is going up." I know it is.

~~~

I will never forget your goofy smile and charm. You've made everyone love you in five months. You touched the lives of everyone here. You touched mine when you made the unicorn mosaic. It was so beautiful, I wanted to buy it from you. There won't be a day when I don't think of you. You were an inspiration.

~~~

My favorite memory was whenever I would hang out with Julie, he would be there clapping his hands on every body part possible. He would clap on Nautica and Ellie. He was a fantastic person. I loved when he did this. He treated everybody so great, and his smile lit up the whole room.

~~~

Can't say I was the closest to Brian Hoeflinger, but I did get to know him a little bit over the past year. Just the few times I talked to him, I could tell he was a really cool, genuine person, and that was evident by all the people there who he had made an impact on. I wished I could have gotten to know him more over the years, but for whatever reason, it never happened. Been to a couple funerals in my life, but never have I been more positive about a soul going to Heaven than I am about Brian. May you rest in peace.

~~~

There is not enough room on this "stupid little card," as Brian would have called it, to describe how much an amazing son, brother, and friend Brian was. He meant more to me than I can ever put in words, and there is no doubt his spirit will live on in me. He was my favorite person to imitate, and I have done so to the point of mastering "The Clap." I will miss Nautica and Ellie, and I will have to visit them if they miss Brian. Imitation is the biggest form of flattery, and there is no doubt in my mind that this is why I caught on to Brian's quirkiness. I love you guys so much, and my heart goes out to you.

~~~

Brian was such an amazing friend and classmate. I will always remember how he made our English class laugh with his great sense of humor. He will be missed by many.

~~~

To someone who could make anyone smile and laugh, and make their day that much better and brighter. To someone who never had a mean thing to say. To someone who enjoyed life to the highest and helped others do that as well. To someone who was a great person.

~~~

I remember sitting at your table in stained glass. Somebody decided to name it the day of insults, but you turned it into the day of compliments. You complimented everyone for the rest of the day, and I could see what a considerate guy you were.

~~~

Unfortunately, I did not know Brian too well, but there is one story about him that truly stuck out for me, and that was when I first met him. It was a few years ago, and I was taking a summer golf camp with my friend Sam. That day, we were randomly paired up with Brian to golf a round of 18 holes. I was not a very strong golfer, and seeing how skilled Brian was at that age was incredible. It wasn't even close when we finished the game, and he showed us what a true golfer was. I saw how passionate he was on the golf course and how he loved to win. Even when he had a hit that wasn't much better than anything I could have done, he was always ready to make the next one better and more accurate. I was grateful for spending that day golfing with him and never knew the impact he would eventually have on my life.

When I heard he was coming to Ottawa Hills, I was excited to meet this kid who I had played golf with so long ago. He may have changed in appearance, but he was still his goofy and passionate self that I remembered. He was always very kind to me and loved to support all the sports that I played. We shared calculus and anatomy class together, and he would always brighten up the room and make people happy. Overall, I am extremely honored to have met Brian and be part of his life, and words cannot describe how sorry I am about what happened. Brian and your family will always be in my thoughts, and I for one will make sure to keep his spirit living.

~~~

I remember you being one of the most spirited individuals in school, going all out for basketball, tennis, and every other sport. You really helped promote school spirit, which brought everyone closer together.

~~~

You have no idea how much I miss your "goofy" personality every day, especially in Psych. I've been thinking about you, buddy. I miss hearing that clap and seeing that wonderful smile. I love you, buddy, forever.

~~~

I first saw you at N. D.'s grad party. This was where I learned you were coming to Ottawa Hills. As we were not close friends, all I have to tell you is my perspective of you as an outsider. I was amazed. Within a short amount of time I saw you make a large number of friends. You had done what most people would have a hard time in any circumstance. You made friends like no other. Also, literally every time I walked past you in the hallway, you had a smile. It's safe to say you made a great first impression. I wish I could be more like you. Fortunately for me, I got to talk to you once randomly out of the blue. Tuesday, January 14th of 2013 after 3rd period calculus (at almost exactly 11:10 a.m.), you struck up a conversation about how you thought our previous lecture on integrals and the fundamental theory of calculus was actually pretty easy and not a big challenge as it was supposed to be. Let me assure you, that stuff is HARD! It was at this point I realized how smart you were. From the word around school I had known you were, but this was proof. I also remember seeing your handwriting once and being very amazed with its perfection. When all is said and done, we miss you very much, but gain comfort in knowing you are in the best of all places. Rest in peace, Brian.

~~~

I don't know why this happened. I don't think anyone will ever know why Brian was taken from us. But what I know is that Brian was placed in our lives for a reason. He was here to be a loving son, caring brother, and kind stranger to anyone he didn't know. Even though I didn't become close friends with Brian, I could tell he had a warm heart and cheerful personality as soon as I met him. We had three classes together—calculus, psychology, and English—and in each one I could see his tremendous work ethic, honesty, and determination to challenge himself. In English, especially, I got to see his goofy side too. We had class after lunch, and he would always walk in with a different bag of candy almost every day. I remember the first time I heard him clap on something—on the window sill behind his desk—and thinking it was one of the coolest things I have ever seen—well, in this case, ever heard. I was lucky enough to sit next to Brian during our class discussions. If I didn't know the answer to something, he was always prepared and willing to help me.

~~~

Our class won't be the same without him. Ottawa Hills as a whole will never be the same. Brian touched all of our lives with his uplifting, positive spirit. Even though he was only at Ottawa Hills for a short time, I will be forever grateful that I had the chance to know Brian. He was truly loved by the Ottawa Hills community and will be forever missed.

~~~

We all miss you so much. Although we were not very close, I still interacted with you on a daily basis. One thing that always impressed me was your determination. Regardless of how much you hated an assignment or felt uncomfortable doing something, you were still devoted to completing the task to the best of your ability. And every time, the best of your ability meant perfection. I hope today you were looking down on all of us with that same goofy smile you always wore. I also hope that you are especially looking down on your family. They are some of the strongest people I have ever met. Kevin, Julie, and Christie would make you so proud. Please know that no one will ever forget you or your amazing, silly, admirable characteristics. We have a

flower behind your seat in English, so you're always with us. Have
some fun for all of us up there. We love you.

~~~

The first time I met Brian was last spring when he was shadowing
here. He immediately seemed like a nice guy, and I had heard of his
golf skills and couldn't wait until tryouts in August. I figured he'd be a
nice addition to Ottawa Hills, but I really had no idea. I remember
watching him play and just being amazed at the amount of talent he
had for the game of golf. More than that, I remember just hanging
around before and after rounds and at the team dinners also. We'd
have some intense touch football games where he had to try hard
because he didn't know any other way. Brian had that charisma that
was untouchable. Everyone knew he was there because of his smile,
and he definitely would have been making someone there laugh. I also
remember cheering on the girls' basketball team with him and Nathan.
He was always so spirited, and I've never seen someone like that for
girls' basketball. However, it didn't matter the sport, because he was
just as spirited at boys' basketball games as well. That win against
Toledo Christian was for you, buddy. We all miss you, Brian!

~~~

The moment I became friends with your son is one I can never
forget. During our first football game, I had happened to look in the
stands when I was coming off the football field. Brian must have not
gotten the memo. While all our Bears were sitting and talking to each
other, almost forgetting that they were at a football game, I noticed
Brian standing up and still cheering. He looked me in the eyes, smiled,
and nodded his head to reassure me he was still watching. We had a

few conversations previous to this, but this was the first time I noticed him. The next day I woke up to take my ACT without any practice or classes. Brian came to mind since I heard he had done extremely well on it. Forgetting that it wasn't even 8:00 a.m., I texted him for advice. What happened next was what made me realize how pure his heart is. One after another, I received multiple texts back with about every bit of information he learned in class. Then it dawned on me that he had just woken up because of me and was not only not mad but went out of his way to help someone he barely knew. To say the least, I miss him. No words can explain how you must feel. Just as no proper words can tell you the amount I would do to change all of this. No part of this is fair. I've lost many friends, but none hurt as much as Brian.

<center>~~~</center>

Wherever you were, whoever you were with, you always had a smile that lit up the room. Your "goofy" attitude towards everyone brought joy to all the people in your life. Not a moment will go by where your loved ones do not think of you. Though your stay in our village was short, the impact you had on each and every one of us was so incredibly substantial. You were an incredible human being, and I and the rest of us love you dearly, and will miss you for the rest of our lives.

<center>~~~</center>

Today is a day that will forever stay in my heart. A day that I will never stop thinking about, no matter what. My best friend since fifth grade, Brian Hoeflinger, has passed away. In life, you really only need very few things to live a happy life. A best friend is one of them. I have been so blessed to have four best friends that I love like brothers. Today, I have three. It is hard to explain what I feel. I hope that none of you ever have to feel this. The fact that I will never see his smiling face again or hear his laugh cuts me deep. I would have to go on and on if I wanted to write all of the good things that Brian did in his life. He was the smartest kid I knew, he could make you laugh even when you felt like nothing could, but most importantly, deep down he had a heart of gold. I will always feel a sense of emptiness. However, I firmly believe this was all part of God's plan. He is an angel now. No more worries, no more stressing. He is carefree in heaven.

Go and find your best friend or friends and give them a hug—not just any hug, but a hug like you have never given them before. Embrace them. Tell them that you love them or how you feel. That is not weird at all. Let me tell ya, I would give just about anything to have my Brian back in my arms, giving him the biggest hug I could possibly give him, and I would tell him that I love him. Life is truly beautiful and can end instantly. You're in paradise now, Brian. Enjoy it, bud. Love you more than you could ever imagine.

~~~

I hope this chapter has provided the insight that each of us has a vision of ourselves that we formulate through life experiences but do not often share with others. On the other hand, how we are viewed by others is a direct reflection of who we feel ourselves to be and how we project this image to the world. Brian certainly presented himself to the world in a fashion which was quite complementary to the person in his writings. He did not seem to put on pretenses, and I think his friends loved and accepted him for that reason. Brian was one of those rare genuine people that others gravitate toward because he did not seem to judge people and instead accepted them for who they were.

I think this quote of Brian's sums it up best:

I promise to never judge a person based upon their appearance. I promise to give every individual I meet an equal chance to become my friend. And I promise to never hate a soul.

Brian was pure of heart in this regard, and his friends recognized it. If we could all follow what Brian wrote in his quote, just think what a better place the world could be!

Chapter 10

Excerpts from My Journals: What Am I Really Thinking?

Often since Brian's death, people have asked me how I am doing. My usual answer is "Good" or "Just fine." I don't tell them the truth, because the truth is quite depressing, and I doubt they really want to hear all that I am thinking. But deep inside each of us, behind the mask we each show to the world, is a trove of thoughts and feelings that most of us will never reveal to others. These hidden thoughts are what define us as truly unique people with real-life experiences. Although we rarely share these guarded feelings in an effort to hide our vulnerabilities, instead choosing to remain on a superficial plane with most people, there is more to us than meets the eye. This is especially true when it comes to our children.

In the past few months, I have had the opportunity to read many of the posts on Facebook which were written to Brian by his friends. The depth of emotion and empathy written in these posts with such articulate clarity was profound, to say the least. Many of these letters are from friends of Brian's who hardly speak when they are around adults. What a world of thoughts they are thinking but only expose or express to the world through media such as Facebook and Twitter. My son Kevin tweeted last night,

5 months has felt like years miss u more than anything Brian.

I feel the same way.

Below is a poem that my daughter Julie wrote for her brother the night he died:

> *I look around for your deep blue eyes*
> *behind them lies an ocean of thoughts*
> *thoughts that could change the world*
> *or thoughts that could change just one person*
> *I look for the spark of determination in*
> *your eyes to make everyone happy*
> *but the room is dark and I am lost.*
> *I listen closely for that goofy laugh*
> *that would light up the room and everyone around you*
> *but the sound of sorrow pierces my ears.*
> *I feel around for your warm beating heart*
> *but I run into a cold hard wall: Reality.*

These discoveries have made me view my children differently since Brian's death. They are very much young adults with thoughts and feelings that are every bit as meaningful as my own. We each think we know our children, but do we? My guess is that we know what they want us to know. They have a whole world that they live in that doesn't involve you, and maybe it shouldn't. On the other hand, this other world is the place where activities such as drinking and drugs are to be found, a place where parents aren't to be and yet need to be for our children's sake. I hope by opening the lines of communication with your children that you might be invited into that secret world of theirs to help them make better decisions for the future. I only wish I could have been privileged into Brian's secret world so that maybe I could have changed what happened to him. For me and Brian, there is no second chance for this to happen. For you and your children, there is still time.

In line with this train of thought, in this chapter I will remove my own mask and reveal to you my deepest thoughts and feelings regarding the death of my son Brian by transcribing for you some of my actual journal notes word for word. I hope by doing so, I can give you insight into the pain and sorrow that comes from losing a child, and an understanding that there is more to each person than meets the eye.

March 2013

It's been five weeks since my son Brian died in a car accident. Still doesn't seem real, but as time moves on, reality continues to solidify itself into my being. I still cannot make sense of it all, and most likely I never will. Cindy and I were quite sad yesterday. The memories can flood into your mind in just an instant, and the awful pain of Brian's death quickly overwhelms you. We were both crying in the den together last evening. As we cried and held each other close, it felt horrible and yet comforting at the same time. The odd thing is that the gut-wrenching pain can overwhelm your body and being for a short moment, and then you feel fine for a while.

What scares me most at this point in time is that my feeling of Brian being real is gradually fading. It becomes harder and harder to remember him walking in the house after school or to hear him talking. The pictures I see of him now are lifeless and do not contain the zest of spirit and aliveness that Brian was every day when he was alive. I hope every day the pain of Brian's loss will continue to ease, but at the same time I do not want to forget the feeling of my son when he was alive. This conflict is constant and torments me on a daily basis. I pace the house often because of the unsettling feeling of not knowing what to do with my feelings and how to let go.

The bottom line is about accepting that Brian is gone from our lives forever in a physical sense. It is this cold, cruel reality that is hardest to face. Knowing that you'll never see or hear someone you loved and who was in your life every day for 18 years is a tough thing to face. To never tell him again face-to-face just how much you love him or how very proud you are of him. There is nothing in my life that comes even close to the pain and agony associated with the death of my son Brian. I have lost my parents and grandparents, which was hard, but does not compare to losing him. I remember my mom once told me after my brother's car accident there was no greater pain than to have a child injured or die. I now know my mom was right! The thing about death is the finality of it. It's the feeling that you cannot change things back to the way they were. It is a split second in time when an event occurs, and everything about that moment changes everything in your life forever. How can anyone accept that? Such an instant in time to change everything! Your mind wants so bad to somehow alter that moment, to have stopped the death, but your heart and reality tell you otherwise.

Nothing can ever, ever prepare a parent for an event like this. Your heart is immediately ripped from your body and left with an all-encompassing void of emptiness. It is a lonely, singular feeling of loss.

I can never forget seeing my son Brian lying there dead on a gurney in the trauma room I have been in so many times before. I can never express in words the feeling of seeing my son lying dead in front of me. He seemed to be sleeping but was never going to wake. I so badly wanted him to wake up, and at the same time I clearly knew he would not. It's amazing what your mind does to you at a moment such as this. Obviously it's a numbing feeling of total disbelief, and at the same time a cruel reality of truth. So you quickly try to bury the feeling of reality to survive. You hope in the morning this was just a bad nightmare that you can will yourself to wake up from. The most painful thing I have ever had to do is to tell my little Kevin, Julie, and Christie that their big brother Brian was dead.

You have to wonder why we are put through such pain, especially at such a young age. What purpose can it serve? What did we ever do to deserve such a stark reality as this?

I can't remember the ride to the hospital much with the kids, but I do remember their reactions once there. They seemed horrified and yet somewhat at peace. I think for them it was a chance to see Brian, touch Brian, and say goodbye to Brian one last time. I think seeing Brian one last time even in the state of death that night made all the difference in the world for our children and their ability to heal. I think having the kids see Brian dead in the ER that night helped solidify the reality of his death. What a cruel thing to say, but that is the truth of the matter. This was their new reality, and I think they have accepted it a lot sooner than Cindy and I ever will as parents. Losing Brian is losing a part of myself. His dreams, hopes, and aspirations all gone, and much of me, many of my hopes and dreams, were lost that night as well.

For weeks after his death, the meaning of life and living was gone. There was nothing to look forward to. Even knowing I still have a great wife and three other wonderful children, life had lost its meaning. This feeling has eased slightly but has certainly not left. How do I ever reconcile a life without my oldest son? He was so much more a part of my hopes, dreams, and life force than I realized when he was alive. How true the saying, *"You don't know what you've lost until it's gone."* Only in death do we realize what an impact someone can make on our lives and the lives of others. This is the place where regret lives and can haunt you indefinitely. All the things I wish I would have said to Brian but never did. I often wonder if he truly knew how much I loved him and how very proud of him I was. If I only had another day to let him know all of this. But that day can never come, which ties back into the feeling of permanency and the inability to alter the past.

I had a friend last night ask me if I, as the father, was staying strong for Cindy and the kids. He wanted to know if I was being strong enough and setting an example to pull our family through this tragedy without falling apart. It was an abrupt question which there was no rote answer to. Cindy and I have not hidden at any point along this road that no one wants to travel. We have always tried to teach our children by example, and this time in our life would be no different. We welcomed people to our home the day of Brian's death to show our kids it is OK to accept the love and care of others. We stood long hours at the funeral where people would wait up to three hours to see us to show our children how others were grieving just like us. I returned to work in some fashion in two weeks to help solidify in my kids' minds that life needs to go on. We set up a memorial fund and two golf tournaments in one month to show our kids that good must come of Brian's death instead of despair. We have always tried to teach our kids by our own example. Cindy and I certainly do our share of grieving. I cry in front of the kids because it's OK to cry when you're hurt and feeling sad. I want them to learn this aspect of life because death, loss, and sadness will always be a part of our life at some point in time. So to answer my friend's question, I told him that I have tried to show strength to my family through my actions and example I set of myself to others. I don't know if this satisfied his curiosity about our situation, but the question did make me reflect on my role as a husband and father.

Another experience of human nature that has moved me is the feeling of helplessness that people have felt over the loss of our son. People innately feel anguish over a loss such as ours and realize there are no words which can ease the pain. Our nature as human beings is to try to comfort and ease the pain of others. Yet in doing so, people feel awkward expressing their grief to us because they realize these are only words and in no way can take away our pain.

A common bond between almost all of us is our children. I believe it is this bond which unifies people in a situation such as this, because it could happen to any of us at any time. For Cindy and me, Brian died and our friends' children lived. It is this stark fact that bonds us together. A future that no one can control or foresee. The uncertainty of life that rules our destiny but is unknown to us until it occurs. And as Brian was quickly taken from us, everyone out there knows it could just as easily have been anyone else. From this experience, I have realized that people do suffer loss even when it doesn't directly involve them.

~~~

I walked into my son's room today. When he first died, I could not bring myself to enter his room alone. The presence of him was too intense and overwhelming to bear. I worried that the continual memories of Brian in our house after his death would overcome the feeling of family we had created thus far. I feared that Brian's death and memories would necessitate us moving out of this house. As time has passed, I am now able to go into his room by myself, but the memories of him in his room immediately encase me and I begin to cry. I look at his shoes lined up along the edge of his bed and his clothes he left in his hamper. His backpack sits there from the last time he came home from school. And then the wave of pain hits that he will never go to school again or return to his room. I can no longer go to his room and ask him how his golf tournament went, or how school was today. No longer can I say good night to him before I go to bed.

The other morning I was sitting on his bed, looking out his window, and for the first time realized that the sun rose over his bedroom each morning. I wondered if he had ever watched the sunrise through his window as I had just done. I can feel and picture how he used to move about his bedroom and lie in bed studying, and all the time I'm wondering how his death can be real. Why should someone as young, vibrant, caring, thoughtful and full of life as Brian die in such a violent car accident? I am always brought back to the question of why.

Everyone has their own thoughts as to why good people die. I have many thoughts but no real answers. Is it a random event, or is it predestined? I do not think we can ever know the answer.

There are some interesting facts that my wife and I have uncovered surrounding Brian's death. Firstly, we found his journals from a retreat he attended at St. John's Jesuit High School this past summer. One of the questions he was asked was, "What are you most afraid of?" Brian's written answer was, "Dying alone in a car accident."

Another fact is that Brian was involved in a fiery car accident the night he died. The first responder at the scene recalled that Brian was unconscious but still breathing with a heartbeat. The car engine was on fire, and rescue personnel were taking turns with fire extinguishers to keep the fire at bay while they were trying to free Brian from the wreckage. The first responder, as he spoke to us in tears, said he decided he "was not going to let this young person die in this car tonight." As five rescuers pulled on Brian and released him from the car, the car immediately burst into flames and was engulfed in fire. We saw the car days after, and the car was incinerated by the fire, including the entire passenger compartment. When Cindy and I saw Brian lying dead in the hospital, he had not one burn mark on his body.

When Brian was in fifth grade, he picked St. Francis as his guardian patron saint. He wore a necklace with a St. Francis medallion, which he rarely removed, especially this past year. He had asked his mom and me within a month of his death if he could get a nicer medallion of St. Francis made of silver. We knew St. Francis was the protector of animals, as Brian loved animals, especially our dogs Nautica and Ellie. In researching further we found, to our surprise, that St. Francis is also the protector of fire and the protector of dying alone.

Is it purely coincidence, or is it destiny that Brian died alone in a fiery car accident and suffered no burns to his body? And is it odd that he had written six months prior that he was most afraid of dying alone in a car accident, and that is just what happened? Is it purely coincidence that his patron saint of his own choosing was St. Francis, who is a protector of fire and dying alone? Can coincidence stretch this far? Again, we can never know for sure.

In addition, Brian's necklace with his St. Francis medallion was cut off his neck that night. We received the chain back, along with his personal belongings, but not the medallion itself. My wife called the ER and spoke with the ambulance personnel. The medallion was not to be found. My wife was frantic because she could not remember exactly what the medallion looked like. She could not remember for sure who the patron saint was. Uncharacteristically, Brian had left his Facebook page open on his computer that day. My wife found he had posted a close-up picture of his St. Francis medallion approximately one year ago on Instagram. She found this picture purely by accident and was able to get an exact copy of the St. Francis medallion Brian had worn, which we then buried with him. What boy posts his patron saint's medallion on Instagram, and why after so many years? My wife believes all of these events were part of a predestined plan for Brian and feels that she was meant to find the picture of the medallion. To take it a step further, she feels Brian somehow sensed his own death and subconsciously posted the medallion picture one year ago so his mother would find it.

You the reader will have to make your own decision on the matter. But I must admit there are a string of events that seem more than coincidence and certainly must reflect some knowledge or understanding greater than our own.

Lastly, on one recent evening while looking through Brian-related letters, my wife found a short letter my daughter Christie had written for a creative writing class. Christie had titled her letter "The Night He Went Away." The letter read as follows:

It was a beautiful night outside on April 27, 1997. I was up until twelve tonight until it happened. CRACK! The lightning outside sounded like it was only five minutes away. That's all I heard, that one lightning strike. The rest of the night was silent and peaceful. The next day I looked and looked, but I couldn't find him. I thought he was gone, but obviously I was wrong.

Ashley, my best friend, and I were playing by the hot dog stand, but we didn't play for long. My mother walked up. "Hi Mom," I exclaimed.

"Where is he?" she asked.

She definitely ruined the fun, but I obeyed and was going to tell her. "Can we at least talk at home?" I asked. We walked home. It wasn't very nice.

I sat down on the couch. "Where is he?" she asked again. I was nervous. The waterfall outside made beautiful music to my ears. "I-I-I," I stuttered. "Uh . . . he is with the street gang," I lied. "He left last night, I think."

"Uh-huh," my mother said.

"I'm going to get an orange," I said.

"No, stay. Don't go into the kitchen," she said.

"Why?" I asked. "All else I know is he is gone."

"That is not fair! He is my baby," my mom exclaimed.

"Then so be it. He could be dead for all I know," I said. "Oh yeah, and one more thing, life isn't always going to be fair. Thomas is gone." After saying those three words, I regretted them right away. I gave up hope. That is not what I live for.

I ran to my room. I looked into my mirror at the tears on my face. I stopped looking at myself and focused on what was behind me. I screamed. I was always told never look back, keep looking forward. Then I realized what I was looking at was the shadow of my dear dead brother. He was smiling as he lay there. My mom was smiling. I was smiling. I woke up. It was all a dream. My dad was in front of me. "Hi, Dad," I said.

"Oh, hi. I bet you were thinking that was a dream," he responded.

"I was," I said. "How do you know about my dreams?"

"I know about your dreams because that wasn't a dream. It was a horrible tragedy."

I looked beside my bed. I saw Tom again. He was dead, but not forever. He will live again someday. The best part is he was still smiling.

As I finished reading the letter, I turned to my wife and asked her what was the big deal about this letter. I said that Christie obviously wrote the letter about the night Brian died, that horrible night we had all lived through on the early morning hours of February 2, 2013. My wife said look again, and I was confused. Christie had obviously detailed the events of that night but had changed the names and added a "creative" flavor to it. She wrote how she was up until midnight when she heard only one lightning "CRACK" only five minutes away and then silence the rest of the night. The accident occurred about five minutes away from our house just minutes before midnight. Several people who heard the crash indicated it sounded like a loud crack or gunshot sound, and after there was silence. She then tells her mom that "Thomas is gone." She runs to her room with tears, after which she looks in the mirror and sees the shadow of her dead brother. She then describes waking up as if it were a dream. Then I show up and tell her it wasn't a dream, it was a horrible tragedy. I still remember standing in our house that night telling our children that Brian had been in a horrible accident and that he was dead. At the end of her story, she acknowledges that Tom, who is her brother, is dead. Much of what Christie wrote in this letter corresponded with the essence of the events of that night. Thus I again reiterated to my wife that she wrote about the night Brian died. My wife then said look at the date. Christie had written this letter in September of 2012, four months before her brother Brian died. I was speechless, and I think that any previous beliefs that I have had in the past about fate and destiny were now changed forevermore. All I could feel at that moment is that there must be more to the universe than we can ever know. How could Christie, my 11-year-old daughter, write about events that wouldn't happen for another four months in the future? Is this yet another coincidence in a series of strange events, or was Brian's death predestined and Christie able to sense this future and subconsciously write about it?

~~~

Today was a long, hard day. I had five surgeries, with my last case a T11 corpectomy for spinal cord compression in a 53-year-old woman with metastatic breast cancer. All five of my surgeries went well, and call was fairly quiet thus far. I've noticed that the feeling of sadness gradually creeps up on you as the day moves on. The memories and thoughts of Brian come to me, and usually I will start to tear up. I was at the scrub sink for my last case and for a fleeting moment it felt like I could go home and Brian would be there. But almost immediately I realized that it's not real, and I started to cry to myself. So I take my time to control my emotions, take several deep breaths, and enter the operating room acting like everything is OK.

My friend called me today on the way home from work to see how I was doing. He said he was in Louisiana on business. He asked how I was, and I told him I had just been crying in the car thinking of Brian. He asked me why I was still so sad six weeks later. I told him that I can't stop all the memories from flooding into my thoughts. When I was in the locker room changing, I looked at my shoes, and it made me think how much Brian loved nice clothes and loved to dress up. Then I felt the anguish that he will never have the chance to dress up nice again. My friend suggested that I try to think of his memories in a positive fashion and not a negative one. I guess that could work, but I cannot rationalize these raw emotions. My son is gone, and I can't forget yet how much I loved him and how much he loved being alive! Brian loved his life. He loved his friends, his family, his dogs, his clothes, his car. He loved to be active. Working out, golfing, playing Spikeball, basketball, going out for a nice dinner. He loved and appreciated it all. And now it's all gone and can never be again. How can anyone cope with that fact? He was too young to die at age 18 when he was really just starting his life as a young adult. I think my friend was trying to help the best he could, but no one can understand my feelings unless you've lost your oldest son as I have. Everyone's life has moved on but Brian's. Brian's dead, and so is a big part of who I am. I never realized just how much of who I am came from my son Brian. Now that he's gone, I feel like an enormous part of me is gone forever. I can never again be the same person I was prior to Brian's death!

~~~

I was on call last night and was up a good deal overnight. The frequent calls keep me from soundly falling back to sleep. And as you do fall asleep, another page comes in, waking you back up. This morning I left for the hospital about 5:45 a.m. Went directly to ICU and saw a 40-year-old male who was intoxicated and struck by a car. Patient suffered a severe C1-C2 distraction injury with compression to upper spinal cord and lower brainstem. Diffuse SAH noted throughout basal cisterns as well. Pt was clinically brain dead to my exam. I spoke with mother and other family regarding his grave condition. I carefully explained what brain death meant. The mother started to cry over her son's morbid condition and appeared to become numb soon after. I did indicate that some good could come of this tragic event and began to discuss the option of organ donation. Soon thereafter, the mother indicated that she would like to donate her son's organs to help others.

Simultaneously, I was paged about a 58-year-old male who was being flown from a rural ER by helicopter with a large intracranial bleed on the left. The patient was comatose and intubated. I spoke with the patient's wife on the phone and discussed treatment options. We decided for emergent surgery when he arrived. When the helicopter landed, pt was taken immediately to CT scanner for a new scan as his neurological status had deteriorated en route. The new CT showed marked enlargement of his bleed. The patient was taken immediately to OR per the family wishes, and surgery was begun. Once the brain was exposed on the left, the blood clot cavity was entered and enormous amounts of blood removed. The brain quickly went from firm and swollen to flat and sunken. Surgery was fairly uneventful, and the patient was transferred to Neuro ICU. Immediately after surgery, I spoke with his wife and nine other family members. I was quite honest in telling them that he was in critical condition and that he had an even chance of surviving vs. dying. The wife and family were very understanding given the circumstances. This was a very difficult case for me. Surgery of this nature is meant for life-saving measures, but survival is often not the best outcome and does not often equate with quality of life.

When I was a teenager, my older brother Eric was involved in a car accident at age 21. He was a junior in college at the time. The accident occurred in the early morning hours, and alcohol was involved with both vehicles. Eric's car was massively damaged, and so was his body. He was taken to an outlying hospital where he was quickly transported by helicopter to the Medical College of Ohio in Toledo, Ohio. Eric had suffered a severe head injury, among other injuries, and required emergent brain surgery that night. Eric survived surgery and remained in the ICU for weeks thereafter in critical condition. We were told that he would most likely die, but he did not. Eventually Eric gradually awoke from his coma approximately six months later. He has required constant care since that time as he cannot walk or talk. He is completely dependent on others. My mother, grandmother, and father devoted the rest of their lives to taking care of Eric, who now lives in a nursing home. Eric survived that night as a result of surgery but with no real quality of life. In addition, our family dynamic was permanently changed by Eric's tragedy and my parents consumed by Eric's dependency on them. Thus, from personal experience, I do not feel that survival is always the best option, and sometimes death is the more humane route. I know that sounds horrible, but only through experience do we learn the truths of life. The family wanted everything done because that is our natural instinct as humans, to want to save a loved one's life. Only in hindsight is this idea of "not treating" a conceivable notion, as the family in the immediate throes of tragedy cannot comprehend such a gesture.

~~~

I have really started to hate Friday nights because that is the night Brian died. As I lay in bed, it is 10:15 p.m. and Brian died six weeks ago this evening. He would have been at a party right now with his friends, having fun. He left the party around 11:45 p.m. and struck the tree in his car about five minutes later. Cindy and I were sleeping at the time Brian died. No chance to stop the event and no chance to say goodbye. Each Friday night I feel I have to stay awake until midnight to somehow acknowledge that it happened or to somehow punish myself for being asleep and not knowing it happened. The sequence of events that night were so specific that I have wondered if this was a predetermined event that was meant to be.

Cindy and I were speaking with a friend of Brian's yesterday. She was telling us that she, Brian, and two other friends were supposed to go out to dinner that night, but Brian and his friend backed out. Instead, they went to Jimmy John's with another friend and, as it turned out, he ended up not eating. Brian had also texted a friend earlier in the evening about meeting her and her friends at Cold Stone Creamery. He wanted to come over, but she told him not to because the lines were too long. She also told us that she was supposed to drive Brian to the party that night but did not have room in her car because of a wheelchair she was taking to the basketball game. So Brian ended up driving his car instead. At the party, several of his friends tried to stop him from leaving and actually had his keys at one point. But Brian eventually got his keys, got into his car, and drove away to his death.

Was this supposed to be his true destiny, or was this purely an accident? That is what's so hard to comprehend. There are so many little circumstances that night that if any one of them could have been different, then the course of the evening would have been changed and Brian would still be alive. Only if? But all the many events of the evening lined up just right, and Brian was killed at 11:50 p.m. in a tragic car accident. I still cannot fathom that my son has died in a car accident. It's not something that I ever even remotely thought could or would happen to one of my children. I always thought Brian would have a great life, have kids, and die at an old age well past my death. His dying the way he did and at such a young age makes absolutely no sense to me. Is there something I should know that I'm not being told? I wish I knew what he was thinking as he drove down the road toward that tree. And why was he driving so fast? And what distracted him to cause him to veer off the right side of the road and strike that large tree next to the woods? How much had he been drinking and why? I guess only Brian would know the answer to the questions I ask. What I am allowed to know is that I will never see my son Brian again in this lifetime. That is the reality that we are left with, and there are no answers as to why. Seems cold and detached to have such an abrupt ending to a wonderful life such as Brian's.

As I am writing this tonight, my son Kevin came into my bedroom and told me that his friend had just kicked a basketball into our outdoor garage light and broke it. Kevin apologized to me for breaking it. I asked him nicely to clean the glass up but told him not to worry about breaking the light. I told him it was OK and we could buy a new one. Prior to Brian's death, I'm sure I would have been quite upset. But now, it doesn't really seem to matter much, because like I said, we can easily buy another one. We can't buy another Brian. He's gone, and nothing can bring him back as long as I live. Some things in life are just not worth getting upset about when you look at the grand scheme of things. Brian's sudden untimely death has really taught me what's important in life, and it's certainly not the material items we constantly gather. I would give up everything I own to have my son Brian back! All material items can be replaced when broken, but not a human being. As a result of Brian's death, I will make a much greater effort to spend more time with my wife and children, because you cannot buy more time once a loved one is gone!

It's now 11:40 p.m., and I can almost imagine Brian leaving the party in his car. He was found with his seat belt on and so had sense enough to wear his seat belt as he always did. In speaking with many of his friends regarding that night, they say he seemed like Brian. He did not seem to be in any unusual mood.

It's now 11:45 p.m., and Brian is most likely driving in his car. I suspect he was driving to his friend's house, which was just down the road from the accident site. He had probably plugged his iPod into his car's stereo system, and I imagine him listening to music as he drives through the darkness, looking forward to getting to his friend's house to most likely spend the night.

It's 11:50 p.m. now, and at any moment Brian's car will have struck the tree head-on at high speed, and Brian's life will have been ended. What a horrible story to have to live over and over for the rest of my life. I hope I can find peace with all of this someday, but for now the daily torment of memories is all I know. Good night.

~~~

Just woke up today with the intense feeling of missing Brian as though it happened last night. That horrible feeling of disbelief that he is gone and never coming back. The feeling that I cannot go on living without him and wondering how I will survive this pain the rest of my life. Can I survive this pain the rest of my life? These are very unsettling feelings that come in waves at certain times, and I feel smothered by them. I try to find a rational way to cope, but there is none. I can only hope these episodes diminish with time because I will never be able to return to a normal life if they do not.

Cindy is up now and reading thoughts and quotes of Brian's off his Facebook account. The boy had a lot of good ideas and thoughts that I never knew or appreciated before his death. Now that he is gone, everything takes on a new meaning to me. This whole experience continually reminds me of the truly important things in life and has taught me not to sweat the small things. What I have been reminded in a sobering way is that life is truly too short to not enjoy the ride. We always hear people say that life is too short and we should live life to its fullest every day. Good thought but certainly hard to do in actuality, or is it?

Cindy was just reading me a post from Brian's Facebook that I would like to share with you regarding a classmate who died in a head-on collision with a semi truck. Brian wrote:

> *Tragedy hits at the most random times, but mainly to just remind us of all the wonderful things we have in this life. Sometimes, it happens to good people, but God chose him for a reason. I didn't know you but you are one of my SJJ Brothers. You and your family are in my prayers along with the prayers of the entire SJJ community. RIP Brother.*

Brian got it! He was learning to appreciate the "wonderful things in life" that we take for granted every day and to not focus on the negative, which brings me to another quote of Brian's. The quote is as follows:

> *By thinking negatively, one will never reach his full potential because he is not allowing himself to fully harness the power of his own mind. Essentially, a person's mindset determines how much they will enjoy the beauty of life.*

Enjoying life to its fullest is right there in front of us every day but can only be realized by how you perceive the day in your mind. You don't have to travel to Paris or climb Mt. Everest to say you have lived life to its fullest. It depends what you perceive in your mind as important. If your children are important to you and you play with them that day, then you have lived a good day. If helping another person is important to you and you do a good deed for another, then you have achieved a good day. I think what Brian was trying to say is that we have so many wonderful things in our lives sitting right in front of us, and often we don't even recognize them.

The best way I can sum it up is that I never realized how wonderful my life truly was and just how much I took for granted every day until I lost Brian suddenly and forever six weeks ago. In retrospect, my life seemed perfect just six weeks ago as compared to my life without Brian now. I will never again worry about what I don't have and will always try to appreciate what I do have. It will probably be the most painful but important lesson that I will ever learn in this lifetime, and it took my son Brian to teach it to me.

~~~

It's 3:30 a.m. I woke up suddenly with a voice yelling "Brian" out loud in my mind. I felt smothered and had to get out of bed. I looked over in bed, and Cindy was gone. I got up and looked for her. I looked in the girls' rooms and saw Julie and Christie sleeping together. I looked in Kevin's room and saw him asleep as well. I walked down to the kitchen and then the den. I looked in all the usual spots she may be late at night, but she was not there. Lastly, I walked into Brian's room where I found her lying in bed with our dog Ellie curled up at her feet. I often don't go into Brian's room because it gives me a feeling of loneliness and sorrow that he is gone. Being in his room seems to solidify the fact that he is gone and never coming back. I guess I'm not at the point that I can let go of him.

Anyway, I lay down in bed with Cindy and put my arm around her. She was awake, and I asked her why she was in Brian's bed. She replied, "Because it makes me feel comfortable." She told me she was reading a book about angels and that everybody has a guardian angel with them. I asked her if this were true, then why didn't Brian's guardian angel save him from the accident? She answered, "Because of free will."

As I listened to my wife talk, I realized how drastically our lives have changed from anything we knew as normal in the past. I feel as though we have entered a new dimension outside of the one we used to live in. A distorted, perverse alternate reality without my son Brian in it. Our lives are now in turmoil, and the whole family is in pain and suffering. Last night we had a fight with Christie because she refuses to do what we ask her to do. She refuses to eat dinner when dinner is ready, and she doesn't want to go to school since Brian died. She refuses to do her homework and won't brush her teeth at night unless forced to do so. It is a constant daily struggle with Christie, and it is wearing on us. Christie is grieving, as are we all. But it's becoming harder and harder to help her when we can't even help ourselves.

People have told us how strong we are. I don't feel strong. I try to get up each day and go to work. I pray for our family to heal and be happy again. I hope for the constant daily pain of Brian's death to go away. If that is what it takes to be strong, then I guess we are strong.

Today in office I saw approximately 35 patients, each with their own set of problems. I try to listen and stay focused, but it takes every ounce of my energy to do so. I continue to think about Brian constantly throughout my day. I struggle with his dying and continually search for the answer as to why he had to die. This quest to find a reason for Brian's death is constant and pervasive throughout my mind. I know that I will never find the answer in this lifetime, but I can't give up because if I give up, I feel as though I am giving up on Brian.

I saw a friend yesterday who knew Brian well. He asked how I was doing and I answered "horrible." I said, "I can't stand the thought of living another 40 years of my life feeling like this." He looked directly at me, and in a calm and slow voice said, "I don't think Brian would want you to feel so sad. He would want you to be happy and enjoy the rest of your life. I truly believe that."

It felt as though Brian were speaking through him. He has known Brian since a child, and I trusted his words. I know what he said is true, and I know Brian would not want any of us to grieve like this over him. But there is some part of me that cannot let go or recede from the pain I am feeling. I continue to pray each day that the pain will lessen and my feelings of emptiness and sorrow be replaced with painless, loving memories of Brian. I talk to people who say this will happen, but I cannot conceive of it right now at this moment. I just saw a picture of Brian when he was younger, and I immediately felt an overwhelming sense of emptiness and started to cry. The thought of never seeing him again after 18 years of his life being intertwined with mine is insurmountable. Why is the pain so different when someone dies as opposed to them moving away? Either way, you don't see the person. But with death there is no chance of coming back, as opposed to moving away, in which there is a chance of moving back. I guess it is the finality of death that overwhelms us. It is the loss of hope that you can never see that person again. Our bodies and souls are geared to differentiate life from death. Why is it not just as easy to celebrate a person's death with thoughts of joy? We know the person who dies would want us remaining on earth to celebrate their life rather than mourn their death. I know in my heart Brian would want this. He would want us to do great things as a result of his death, to use his loss as a catalyst to achieve a greater good for others. But I cannot change the way I feel any more than I can change the fact that Brian is dead. My emotions cannot be rationalized despite how hard I may try, and thus I am left with this ongoing pain for now.

~~~

Kevin and I went and worked out at Wildwood yesterday. We used the TRX workout system with a trainer. This is the first time back to Wildwood since Brian died. We were supposed to work out together at 5:30 p.m. the night he died. I asked him if he was going while he was standing in the kitchen next to the refrigerator. He said he couldn't because he was going out to eat with friends and then going to the varsity basketball game later. I thought no big deal, but little did I know that would be the last time that I would ever talk to him. So many things I would have liked to have told him that I never did. I often wonder if he would have just come and worked out with me that night, if he would be alive today. The problem was he was growing up and wanted to be with his friends. That is why I didn't make a big deal of it. Kevin and I had a good workout together, although I was sad thinking of the times Brian and I worked out. TRX workouts were really the last thing that he and I did together as father and son.

I can't stop thinking and feeling how different my life is now. As I sit here writing this, looking out the window into our backyard, I see the barren trees standing in the cold. They stand there still and seemingly without life. As I stare out the window at this scene, I feel numb and lifeless. My motivation is gone. I hope as winter passes and gives way to spring that I will start to feel like a person again. Someone who can smile and feel happiness and joy as I once did not so long ago. That time seems so far and distant to me right now. We are going to Grand Cayman for vacation over spring break, a vacation we planned one year ago when Brian was still alive. I think the kids are really looking forward to this vacation. I hope that I can, too.

~~~

Just finished rounding at Toledo hospital this a.m. I think of Brian all the time. I looked up his ER notes from the night he died. He was pulseless with no blood pressure upon arrival to TTH. It sounds like he was that way at St. Anne's hospital as well, but I've not looked at those records yet. Horrible feeling to read your son's name, Hoeflinger, Brian Jr., and "expired" next to it. Still extremely hard to believe this has all happened. One thing with Brian's death is that I no longer fear dying, because if I die then I will see Brian again. Hopefully I will live to an old age, but if I do not, I will not necessarily be disappointed. My life has changed that much.

The Alcohol

More details have come out regarding the kids and their drinking. We spoke to the boys who were with Brian the night he died. They came to our house to pick up Brian and drove to the liquor store. All three went in and together bought a 1.75-liter bottle of Belvedere vodka. No one was carded. They then went to the varsity basketball game, where we saw Brian having fun over in the student cheering section. After the game, they went to a friend's house and started drinking out of their vodka bottle. Sounds like they all got drunk. Brian eventually left in his car intoxicated and died soon thereafter.

What bothers me the most is that Brian never let onto his drinking. I suspected he did a little bit here and there, but I would have never guessed he was drinking as much as he was and with hard alcohol. Did we give him too much freedom and he took advantage? Was there peer pressure? Brian always seemed so confident in himself and didn't seem to care about what others thought. So I find it hard to believe that his drinking was all about peer pressure and trying to fit in. I think the drinking was a new experience for him, and he was having fun with it. He just didn't know how to limit and control it. Obviously he is not alone in this regard. Nonetheless, drinking has cost Brian his life and has drastically affected ours. I will never feel the same about alcohol and drinking as long as I live. Should I have talked to him more about alcohol, and would it have made a difference? These are questions that will haunt me for the rest of my life. Of course, we will not make this same mistake with our other children.

Then I have to wonder, why Brian? Drinking is such a big part of our society, and so many people drink and drive. But only a select few die from it. Is it a random incident or a preselected reminder of the dangers of alcohol? Brian was such a good boy and didn't deserve to die the way he did. He did so much good in the world. When thinking of Brian, alcohol was the least of who he was. Then why should he die from something that represented him the least? It makes no sense to me why he should die at all at such a young age with so much potential to bring good to the world. There is no logic in death. We live from day to day never really thinking that we may die until our older years. And most of the time that is true, but for a select few, death comes all too soon and without warning. Do I think Brian knew he was going to die? If he did, he sure didn't act like it. And that's what makes me the saddest and hurts me the most, is that Brian didn't want to die. He wanted to live, go to college, get married, and have kids. He wanted to continue to experience the excitement and fun of life, not to vanish suddenly one night. Sure, people are all heartbroken immediately after you die, but then life moves on and gets back to normal, except you're no longer here. You become a memory but are no longer an active part of people's lives. Once your physical being is gone, you can only be a memory. For the family left behind, we want more than a memory. We want Brian back so we can talk to him again, spend time together again, and watch his life move on as ours will. I can't stand the continued thought of never seeing Brian again. After 7 weeks, I continue to think of him constantly, and I don't know how to stop this continual pain. I still cry frequently and feel a deep sense of aloneness, as though no one can reach me in the depth of my despair. I don't know why I feel this way, but I do, and it takes all my physical and emotional energy to fight off this emotion. I hope someday I can feel happy for Brian and not feel as though he is sad because he had to leave this world and our lives way too soon. And I wonder if I would feel better if I had had the chance to say goodbye to him.

~~~

Just got back from watching a movie at Franklin Park Cinemas with Kevin. As we were driving home, I became very teary and sad. I really enjoyed the movie and realized that Brian would never be able to enjoy a movie again. As we drove down Talmadge Road, I was looking at the yards and houses pass by and thinking how Brian will never experience a ride home again or appreciate the surroundings as he drives down a road. I seem to pay attention now to things that I wouldn't have prior to his death. I'm wondering if I was sad because I enjoyed something that Brian will never have the chance to enjoy again. I can't say I feel guilty, but it's more of a feeling of hurt and sadness.

I was thinking on the way home how our senses are limited to our human experience as physical beings. We expect after death that we will know who we were and maybe even remember the things from our life. But is that possible out of our physical bodies? I wonder if we will be aware of who we were and who we loved in life as we in life know now who we are and who we love? Or are we to experience an aura of satisfaction and love with no recollection of our time on this earth? It saddens me to think that Brian may not remember us and how much we love him! For me, that is going to be the hardest thing to get over. If I knew that Brian was happy and didn't feel the awful loss that I feel, I could feel much better about the future without him. I wish that I could get a tangible sign that would convince me of that. I think that I can handle my loss fairly well, but it's Brian's loss that bothers me so. He seemed so happy in life, and I want him to be just as happy in death. If I had to lose him, I need to know that he is OK in the afterlife. I don't want him to feel alone and without us. I need reassurance like a young child needs reassurance from their parents. I yearn for Brian to let me know he is all right without us. It must be the parental instinct that is driving this intense feeling in me. I know the key to enjoying my life again is to find peace in knowing that Brian is at peace with what has happened to him. I try to find a way to rationalize this, but there is none. I'm hoping that someday it will just come to me.

Brian wrote on May 7, 2012, about an SJJ student's death. He said,

Tragedy hits at the most random times, but mainly to just remind us of all the wonderful things we have in this life. Sometimes it happens to good people, but God chose him for a reason.

If Brian truly believed this, then maybe this is part of his message to me. He also wrote about a hypothetical scenario for a school project discussing if he were to die tomorrow. He said,

I'd want my death to bring good memories and an appreciation for life, not just sadness and tears.

Maybe this is the other part of Brian's message left for me to tell me he is OK. I would like to think so, but I am not yet convinced. For now, I will wait and hope for a more definitive sign.

~~~

This morning as I start my day, my eyes feel very heavy and I am tired. Tired physically and tired mentally. Each day seems a struggle to survive. I feel empty and alone. I can't get the loss of Brian out of my mind. I can't envision how people get over a tragedy like this. To have someone in your life for 18 years and then to have them permanently disappear in a night. I wonder how can life ever feel normal again. To look forward with enthusiasm seems like a distant past. The meaning of life seems like it has been grotesquely ripped from me, leaving me to feel like an empty shell. I know these sound like dramatic statements, but it is how I feel inside.

April 2013

It's been two months since Brian's death, and the feeling of him is gradually fading. I am losing what it felt like to have him around every day and certainly hate the feeling. It is a feeling of helplessness to stop the inevitable. I still cry but not as much these past few days because we are on spring break in Grand Cayman. A change in scenery out of our house and change in our daily routine has made a difference for now.

The days leading up to our vacation were horrible for me. Very emotional and very sad. Our first family vacation without Brian. As I was packing our scuba equipment at home the day before our vacation, I couldn't get everything to fit in our luggage as I have always been able to do so in the past. I was crying, frustrated, and felt like I was having a nervous breakdown. The thought of leaving without Brian was overwhelming and unbearable. Finally I had to stop, and I broke down into a child-like cry so intense that I could hardly breathe. I wanted someone to comfort me and take the pain away as my mom would when I was a little boy. Cindy came over and held onto me while I sobbed in a chair out in the living room. I could barely eat that day. I remember shaking at the kitchen table, my hands trembling as I tried to eat a bagel sandwich. I have rarely felt like that in my life. A feeling that I cannot make something better and just make it go away.

I know this will be a pain that I am going to live with forever. I watch the world around me and see how life moves on. I watch my friend Bill on our vacation, and for him, life has not stopped. He is having fun like a normal person would on vacation, seemingly unaware that life has changed drastically for Cindy and myself. Deep down I know that he knows our loss, but more in a factual sense. He seems very matter-of-fact about moving on. For us, the only matter-of-fact at this point is that Brian is dead. I still cannot move on because it doesn't feel right. I'm sure Brian would want us to have fun on vacation, and I'm trying, but it certainly is not easy. Everything reminds me of him. The problem is how to live life without him. I ask these questions hoping for a logical answer, but there is none. It's all a matter of feeling from your heart that drives your mindset. As the heartache subsides, the ability to think more clearly grows. I'm tired and not making much meaningful thought so will stop for now.

~~~

What if I wasn't here tomorrow?

I would be sad to leave everyone I love but joyous to see my son Brian again! I would miss the warmth of the sun and a gentle breeze on a nice spring day but hope the glow of heaven feels even better. I know the agony of the ones left behind. I wish I could turn that pain into a loving remembrance without regret. As losing a child is certainly the most painful process I have experienced in this life, I feel even more remorse that my son Brian was not ready to die. If I only knew he was at peace, then I could more readily move on with my remaining life. Brian once wrote that "life is the most precious thing to human beings." I hope where he is right now feels like the most precious place to him, and I hope he does not feel regret or remorse about being gone.

Being gone. What a profound two-word phrase. Being gone sounds like not to exist. To not exist draws a feeling of emptiness. Thinking of emptiness brings feelings of sadness. But Brian did exist. He was a happy young man full of life, not emptiness or sadness. So if that is how Brian was in life, why should I think he would be any different in death? He was a very positive person and would want us to be positive. He was happy, and I'm sure would want us to be happy. This all makes sense, but on the other hand, it is so, so hard to let go of Brian from this world. It's a selfish emotion to want someone because they made your life so much better and happier. The joy that he brought to my life, although I didn't fully appreciate at the time. How I will miss the time we spent together playing and watching golf, as well as enjoying a meal on Inverness's patio.

As I try to comprehend the overwhelming effect Brian's death has had on me, I realize how much of me was in Brian. In retrospect, I realize how many of my traits were in him. His sense of competitiveness and wanting to be the best at something. The drive to follow through and finish something you have started. His kindness, politeness, and respect toward people. All traits I am so proud of him for because they are part of who I am. Brian was his own person, and yet he was me. That's why a part of me has died, because Brian was a part of me forged over 18 years. I was so proud of him, and I feel a deep sense of guilt that he will never have the chance to complete his dreams as I have. Why did Brian lose his chance to complete his life and dreams?

I so wish I could talk to him to see how he is doing. To ask him how his day was and ask him if he misses us. To let him know just how much I love him and would give anything to have him back here at home. Our family will never be the same without him. I hope God is taking care of Brian and shielding him from the same pain we are feeling here on earth. I hope most of all that I will see Brian when I die and be able to interact with him as I did when he was alive. This world is all I know, and my interactions with Brian are all based in this world. I miss the physical and emotional connections, because this is all I have reference to here on earth. How will my interaction with Brian be after this life? That's something I will not know until I die, but it is certainly something I will think about for a long time. Until then, I have to figure out how to move on with life and let the feelings of sadness and remorse go. *I love you, Brian, and don't ever forget that, because I will never forget how much I love you! Love, Dad.*

~~~

Cindy and I gave a talk to the St. Ursula students yesterday regarding teens and alcohol. We had a video presentation and slides as well. It was overwhelming to watch a video summarizing your son's life, including his death, in front of an entire school. I was crying and shaking as we watched the pictures of Brian's crashed car go by. And that is what it now feels like, that his life has come and gone by. Eighteen years in the blink of an eye, and now he is gone forever. I think the finality has set in, and our lives can never be the same.

I'm sitting here alone in the great room, writing this passage. All the kids are gone and out doing things. The house feels empty and lifeless. Since Brian has been gone, there is a stillness about things. Cindy and I went to a movie last night. All the kids were again out doing things with friends. Everything seems so much quieter and less energetic since Brian's death. I think Cindy and I are starting to feel an aloneness and sadness, which makes me wonder how things will be when the other kids start leaving for college. I feel an air of emptiness to our house, with Brian's essence trapped inside as a reminder. An all-encompassing memory of the love we had in our lives as a family with Brian, but only to haunt me as a desire to change things back to the way we were. But in a second, Brian was taken from this world, and our lives never to return to normal. At first you want to ignore it and pretend it didn't happen. Then you feel angry that it did happen, as if the anger will serve some purpose to bring him back. In the end, you are left only with the reality that he is gone from our lives, and all the precious moments that may have come will never be!

Life seems very cruel and unfair. But what is fair? Is death unfair, or is it a preplanned step to another stage of your spiritual life? Maybe some people are ready sooner than others for this transition. But does that mean that they want to leave early? And what of babies and young children who don't even know what they could possibly want? Death at an early age does not make sense for me. Brian thought God chooses good people for a reason. He believed that, and I certainly hope he was right, because I would hate to think Brian's death was a random event with no reason or purpose to it.

Or do we, the living, make the reason and purpose from an untimely death? We have created a fund and golf tournament in Brian's name and started to give talks on alcohol and teens, all to benefit someone else from Brian's tragedy. We are creating new meaning and purpose from his death, but I can't believe he died just so we could carry out this mission. Could Brian have died for the greater good of others? I guess that's possible, but it doesn't seem fair to Brian. I guess we will never know while we are living. And once we are dead, it doesn't seem we are able to reach back to the living to give an answer.

For now, I will try to keep my memories and love for Brian alive and as fresh in my mind for as long as I can. I will try to make as much good come from his death as I can. But in the end, I will always be continually haunted by the stark reality that my son Brian is never coming home to see me again in this lifetime.

~~~

Couldn't sleep tonight. Thinking about my son Brian. It is 12:50 a.m., just about the time he was pronounced dead at Toledo Hospital ER on February 2, 2013. I remember the intense pain of that night and the sheer disbelief that Brian was gone from our lives forever. In a fleeting moment he died while Cindy and I were asleep, never to have a chance to say goodbye to him. The pain of Brian's death has lessened slightly but is certainly not gone. There isn't a moment of any day that I still don't think about him in some fashion, whether it is a vivid memory or just an intense feeling of loss or longing for him.

I was thinking today how I used to look forward to the weekend and how excited I would be on a Friday afternoon to get out of work early. The excitement and enthusiasm are gone. Life is so different now. It's like Cindy and I go through the motion of living each day but almost without true purpose and meaning. I guess this is because a big part of our purpose in life is gone forever. Our children play such an enormous role in our happiness and well-being as parents. They bring happiness and purpose to our lives. When a child dies, you feel a particular loss of purpose and well-being. The excitement and zest of life is extracted from you in a sudden instant. I don't think I will ever look forward to life again in the same way as I did when Brian was alive. The permanency of loss is a horrible feeling. It haunts you every day as a constant reminder of what you once had and what you will never have again. This is why death in any fashion, regarding anyone at any age, is so hard to accept, because of the permanency of death.

The other night I was called in to see an elderly man who fell and struck his head on the ground. He was brought to Toledo Hospital where he was comatose, requiring a breathing tube. The CAT scan of his head showed a very large blood clot on his brain. By exam, he was comatose with evidence of permanent brain damage. He would not survive without surgery, and even with surgery there was a high likelihood he may never wake up. The family had a very difficult decision to make. Should they let him go and let nature take its course, or not let go and intervene with surgery? The toughest part of this decision-making process is accepting that the man has suffered permanent brain damage and will never be the same even if he were to survive. It is accepting the fact that something in your life has changed permanently, and from that moment forward, things can never be the same despite your intense desire to change things back to the way they were. I think the finality of death is the hardest part of letting go and moving forward with life. Of course, it is the hardest part of reality to deal with, and some people ultimately cannot accept the loss of a loved one and cannot move on with life.

What I have just written seems like a rational approach to thinking about death. But what you actually experience with loss is intense emotional pain, which is not based on a rational thought process. So this is where the dichotomy lies. You cannot rationalize death, because it is an emotional experience. With time, emotions subside, and hopefully life begins to move on. I hope this is true for us, but it has not happened yet.

Only after Brian's death three months ago do I now realize just how perfect my life really used to be. As the saying goes, you don't realize what you have until it is gone. It is such a true statement. We certainly love our three other children, Kevin, Julie, and Christie, with all our hearts, but life will never be the same without our son Brian in it. A tremendous amount of good is resulting from Brian's tragedy. Even so, as parents and a family, Brian is gone from our lives forever. And there is no ultimate amount of good that can be done to replace the loss we have felt over Brian. I know everyone understands that, but I need to say it for Brian's sake. There is no way to ever express in words how much we miss him and just how drastically our lives have changed forever without him.

And yet most importantly, beyond the tangible items noted above, there is the intangible appreciation for our remaining family and children. Brian's death has forced me to re-evaluate what is most important in life, and certainly that is my family. I am trying to spend more quality time with them and trying harder to talk one on one with each of my kids, which is not always the easiest thing to do with teenagers. Trying to get to know each of them better and ensuring that they know how much I love each of them. In the end, I have gained a better insight into and appreciation for what is truly important in our lives. I think we need to frequently remind ourselves of that, because all too often we take things for granted. And we know how quickly life can change. You can wake up one morning and a loved one is gone forever, leaving you no chance to redo things a second time. So you have to make the first go-round count every day and be content with your actions or lack of actions thereafter.

June 2013

I hurt so very much today. The overwhelming feeling of sadness has not been this intense as of late. We went to the Ottawa Hills High School senior graduation last night. Being there didn't feel right without Brian. I felt inside that we shouldn't have been there. Our family was asked up on stage to accept an honorary diploma for Brian. Initially there was deafening silence, followed by uncontrollable clapping. It was a nice gesture, and I appreciated it. But even this was unsettling to me. It was yet another reminder of what we have lost. A whole lifetime of hard work and commitment gone because of a night of senseless drinking. Brian was always so proud of his grades, and he received no recognition at graduation for his outstanding academics. There were five summa cum laudes brought onto stage, and Brian could have been one of them.

I continue to live in disbelief of his dying. How a life can grow so wonderfully for 18 years with so much gifted promise for the future, and suddenly it's all gone in an instant. How can one ever reconcile with that? My answer is you can't. I may be forced to live with it, but I will never fully accept his death. I was in his room earlier, crying inconsolably. All his personal belongings sitting there, his trophies, clothes, and shoes in his closet, toiletries in his bathroom. All reminders of the life he used to have. A wonderful, accomplished life that no longer exists. People tell me that Brian will live on in memory and spirit, but that doesn't make me feel better as a father who lost his first child and his oldest son. Brian is a reminder of my accomplishments and the dreams that I had at his age. As every parent would want, I wanted Brian to have a chance to fulfill his dreams and enjoy a long life. The fact that he can never do that is what hurts me the most. It is a horrible pain that nags at you at every waking moment. The overwhelming sense of loss smothers any thoughts of happiness or joy.

I came home from work today. It's Friday and I'm off for the weekend. But I look forward to nothing. No feeling of excitement or anticipation. Just a feeling of sadness for the loss of Brian.

~~~

Played golf with Kevin today at Inverness. Very emotional round. So many memories and emotions all at once, walking from hole to hole and remembering all the shots I watched Brian make. It was like walking with a ghost through the course. All the time I spent with Brian through the bouts of anger and development of his game, to the point of him finally starting to master and enjoy the game. He was finally appreciating his talents and accepting his limitations as they may be. He was growing up and no longer an impetuous kid. Our time together with golf had matured him to an adult level. I so miss that. All the years of investment from both of us had finally paid off. And now in an instant, it's all gone.

Golf will never be the same again for me. I hate that feeling of loss when you realize you have lost something that you can never have back again. What was the purpose of Brian's life? All his hard work over the years, all the life he lived and wonderful things he did in 18 years, and for what? To die in a senseless car accident? What was the purpose of his life, and why did we lose him at such a young age? Nothing makes sense to me.

It's Friday again, and I look forward to nothing. I used to be so excited about the weekend, particularly the chance to play golf. That is gone from my life now. There is no more excitement or anticipation for things to come. I try to get by each day but with no sense of fulfillment. My life continues to feel empty without Brian in it. I know that statement is not fair to my remaining family, but it is how I feel at the present time, and I don't know how to change it. I can only hope time will bring joy back into my life.

~~~

Life has improved slightly since I've written these entries. Five months have passed since Brian's death. I am now able to smile and occasionally look forward to a night out. But many of the feelings that I have shared with you remain with me on a daily basis. I have come to live with them each day but certainly have not accepted them fully. I now realize that this horrible event that we are living through will never leave our presence completely. There will always be a place of emptiness and sadness where Brian brought joy and happiness.

You have just journeyed through the worst months of my life. I can only hope that this experience has heightened your appreciation for life and for the loved ones which surround you. I also hope that the raw emotions revealed to you in this chapter will inspire both parents and children to talk openly and honestly with each other, particularly regarding the topic of alcohol and substance abuse.

Brian once tweeted:

So excited. Can't wait to see what the future holds for me.

That future no longer exist for Brian. Please don't surrender your future needlessly. Learn from Brian's mistake, as every decision you make in life, right or wrong, has a direct consequence and affects not only yourself but those around you in ways that you can never foresee.

Chapter 11

Where Do We Go from Here?

I woke up this morning thinking of something Brian tweeted in the months prior to his death:

> *Just remember when times are at their worst,*
> *things can only get better.*

There is no reference to the context in which he was speaking, just the quote. As I thought about this statement, it felt as though Brian was coaching me not to give up during this low point in my life. We don't know exactly where our lives will take us from here, but who really does? It seems like I live from day to day with little ability or desire to plan my future as I have always done in the past.

I walked into my son's room this morning before leaving for work. As I sat on the edge of his bed, I thought to myself that this is my son Brian's room. I have a son named Brian who is a wonderful young man. But at the same time, I also know he is dead and never coming back to this room. I wish you could appreciate the pain in this statement—the anguish which is caused from transitioning from the present tense to the past tense as I speak of a human life, my son's life. I hate what has happened to our lives.

I am standing in the hospital hallway on a Sunday morning as I write this passage. I wonder what is in store for us next. Is there another tragedy in our future, a future that we cannot control? It's a scary thought for anyone, but it is reality. I remember in the months prior to Brian's death how good life was. I was happy and having fun. I was exercising and running every day. I felt as healthy and alive as I ever have in my life. Since Brian's death, I have not exercised or gone for a run. It's been five months, and I cannot bring myself to do so. I mentally cannot resume these activities because it brings on feelings of when I was happy and Brian was still alive. It hurts too much to remember that time of happiness. I guess I feel this way because Brian no longer has a chance for happiness, at least in the way that I can comprehend it.

I feel as though these words I'm writing cannot be true. Brian should be here with us. This is a unifying theme in my life as it stands now, and a unifying theme in my wife's life, too. I talk to my children about Brian's death. They share their thoughts briefly, but it does not seem to have affected them in the same way it has affected Cindy and myself. I often think of all the other people in this world who have had a loved one die and other parents who have lost a child. Can all these people be feeling the same excruciating pain and sense of loss that I do? I know the answer is yes, but still I feel such a singular loss that it seems like no one else could relate to it. It is this feeling of aloneness that has been the hardest emotion to cope with, because with loss comes a feeling of emptiness. How do I now fill my life back up with happiness? If I somehow knew the answer to this question, life would make a lot more sense.

~~~

After I finished my rounds at the hospital, I took Kevin over to a friend's house, the same friend's house he was picked up from the night Brian died. As I drove back home, I stopped by St. Joseph's school, where Brian attended kindergarten through eighth grade. The school has planted a fir tree in memory of Brian. As I stood with this small tree in the rain, I read the plaque at its base, which reads:

Brian Hoeflinger

St. Joseph Class of 2009

"Even the smallest of accomplishments is greatly appreciated in the eyes of a positive person because it is another step in the right direction."

As I stood there alone in the rain facing this tree, I asked myself, *Why did it have to be my son?* That one question will never go away. But as I thought about Brian's quote on the plaque, I realized that maybe I was looking at things the wrong way. Instead of thinking about what I have lost, could I try to focus on the positive and what I have gained? Instead of dwelling on what I will never have again, maybe I should try to look at what good I can do in the future. Maybe in this fashion, I could someday look forward to life and happiness again.

As I reflected in front of this young but growing tree, I felt an old door slowly closing in my life and a new one beginning to open. I knew that I had to let go of the past to move forward into the future. But letting go of the past makes me feel like I am letting go of Brian.

As I continued to look at this young tree, I thought of what it represented. It is planted in a spot in front of the school where all kids will walk by on their way into school each day. The tree will stand there as a testament to a young person who once was happy and full of life, a young man who brought a smile and joy to so many lives, who was so positive that people gravitated toward him to tap into his uplifting energy—one of these rare, special individuals who brought people together with his infectious enthusiasm. As this tree stands there through the years, it will serve as a beacon to this life which was once Brian Nicholas Hoeflinger.

This was the moment when I decided to move forward with my life, using Brian's energy as my guide. Although I can't fully explain it in words, this feeling that had been slowly building in me solidified as I stood in front of this unassuming yet humbling tree. Maybe Brian was there this day. I can't explain why I drove to the school to see the tree, but I can tell you I felt compelled to do so even though it was raining and not on my way home.

Some people have told me that Brian will come to me at the most unexpected of times. I have waited months for a sign, but none has yet to appear. I have read of people being visited by their dead loved ones, but I have not yet been visited. Maybe this was my first true sign from Brian, a message for me to move on to the next chapter of my life, whatever that may be. A message to let me know it is okay to move on and be happy again. A message to say that he is okay and will be there waiting for us as the years pass by, as this tree will stand there through the years, waiting for students to walk by and remember Brian.

There is another tree as well: the mature oak that received the impact of Brian's car and bore witness to his life and his death. It serves as a living monument to all who pass by of the fragility of life.

As I am now learning, it is time to focus on Brian's life and no longer on his death. So much good can come from this horrible event which you now bear witness to. Not only should we learn from Brian's mistakes regarding alcohol, but we should learn from his life and the goals he set for himself as well. Brian once wrote,

Striving to achieve a goal is part of everyone's life at some point. Goals are not easily attained, however, and some are more difficult to reach than others. I have come to realize that all goals are indeed attainable, but not all goals are easy to achieve. Hard work and precious time is required to reach what at first might appear to be the sky. The most important thing to understand when referring to achieving a goal is that it will not happen overnight; a goal requires so much more than that.

Brian lived his life by this philosophy, and he went far in his short 18 years of life. To this end, I want kids to see what accomplishments they could achieve as Brian did, if only they set their minds to it—to realize the potential each and every one of us has embedded within ourselves, just waiting to be discovered, and to realize how each decision we make can affect not only our own lives but so many of the lives around us. Never feel like you are not loved, because you are. As Brian once said,

> *It's not over till you give up, and even then it's not over because you've still got so many people who love and care about you.*

Never forget this message, and never underestimate yourself, as you have so much more to offer the world than you could ever imagine. It took the death of my son Brian to make me truly understand this.

Lastly, please take the time to tell your family, particularly your children, how much you love them and how proud you are of them, because you never know if you will have that chance again.

As to what the future may ultimately hold for us, only time will tell. When I'm on call and in the Toledo Hospital ER, I often stop in trauma bay 24, the room where Brian was pronounced dead. I stare at the empty gurney and picture Brian lying there dead with a breathing tube in his mouth and the white sheet covering his body up to his neck. As I relive those hideous moments, I am reminded that time reverses for no one. Time, the most precious commodity that we all own, is finite and cannot be bought or sold. It is a limited numerical measurement of our existence here on earth, a true reminder that we must spend this unknown allotment of time wisely and with the ones we love, because, as I have learned firsthand in the most horrible of ways, the future is unpredictable, can be cruel, and changes for no one.

In closing, I would like to share an exchange that I had with a very nice woman the other day. She is an elderly patient that I was consulted to see while on call, who takes blood thinners for a heart condition. She had fallen and struck her head on the ground, resulting in a thin blood clot over her brain. No surgery was required, just observation in the ICU. On my second visit with her in the hospital, she said to me that we both had something in common. I asked her what it was, and she answered that we had both lost a son. I told her a bit about Brian and his life, and she shared a little information about her son. She reiterated to me what I have been told so often before, that you never truly get over the loss of a child. The pain will ease and you will learn to live with it, but the loss will always be there.

As we concluded our brief conversation, the woman turned to me and asked directly, yet softly, "What will be Brian's legacy?"

She caught me off guard. There were so many things I wanted to say regarding the matter. While she waited patiently, I took a moment to reflect on Brian's life, then responded, "I think Brian's legacy to the world would be for every person to strive to be their personal best by not only believing in themselves, but giving of themselves for the betterment of another." This is the true measure of a person, and my son Brian realized this important life lesson prior to his death. I hope he will now be remembered for this ideal after his death.

We will all leave a legacy someday when we die. When our own legacy is called into judgment, we can only hope that the path we led in life has contributed to the world in a positive direction.

The night he died, Brian made a mistake, and that one mistake cost him his life. That is the harsh reality of teenage drinking. And yet from this tragedy has come guidance and hope for others not to make the same mistake. It is this retrospective reflection on life and the experiences contained within that life that ultimately bring wisdom and change for the future. I hope that the life experiences exemplified in this book will bring about positive change for all to benefit from someday.

In Loving Memory of our son,
Brian Nicholas Hoeflinger
12/28/1994 – 2/2/2013

A heart of gold stopped beating, two shining eyes at rest.
God broke our hearts to prove he only takes the best.

Appendix 1

Lessons Learned: What Every Parent and Teenager Should Know

In May 2013, we were asked by the *Toledo Free Press* newspaper to write a letter to the graduating class of 2013 regarding teenage drinking. My wife and I wrote the letter together, and the *Free Press* made it their front-page article the week before graduation. Within days, the letter went viral on the Internet and has been opened online over 1.5 million times as of August 2013. I then wrote a follow-up letter to all teenagers, which the *Free Press* again printed. As of this writing, the second letter has been opened online over 700,000 times. I have since written a third letter to parents, which again was published and after two weeks was viewed over 350,000 times. Each of these letters offers insight and opinions from Cindy and myself, the parents of a child who died as a result of teenage drinking.

The response to these letters has been overwhelming. Cindy and I are frequently stopped by parents and students to thank us for writing them. We have found that many parents are using the letters as a vehicle to open the lines of communication with their children regarding the topic of alcohol. This chapter is dedicated to the content of these three letters in their entirety.

Letter #1

Brian Hoeflinger: The Harsh Reality of Teenage Drinking

To the graduating class of 2013:

Our son Brian Hoeflinger died in a tragic car accident on Feb. 2 at the young age of 18.

He was a kid just like you who had hopes and aspirations of going to college and having a full, happy life.

On the night he died, he was at a party with friends drinking vodka and ended up driving intoxicated. I remember the phone call we received late that night when we learned Brian had been in a car accident. The sickening feeling in the pit of your stomach and the frantic racing of your heart when you don't know if your child has been hurt or if he is even still alive.

When we arrived at the hospital, we were told Brian was dead. The image of our son lying there on a cold gurney dead in trauma room 24 at Toledo Hospital will never leave my mind as long as I live. His lifeless body lying there almost as though he were asleep, wishing he were only asleep, but knowing he was dead and never coming back home with us. It is the worst singular feeling we have ever experienced in our lives.

The second worst feeling was telling our other three children at home about an hour later that their older brother Brian was dead and gone forever. We took them back to the hospital to see Brian. It was heartbreaking to watch Kevin, Julie and Christie say goodbye to their big brother forever that night. That life we had with Brian is over and an unwelcome new life without Brian has now taken its place.

We tell you this story because Brian could be any one of you, if you choose to drink. And we say choose, because it is your choice and nobody else's. Once you take your first drink of alcohol, you are not making the decisions, the alcohol is. You are putting yourself and others at risk for injury, or even worse, dying like Brian.

Now you may say that Brian was stupid and not a responsible person. You would never make that mistake and it could never happen to you. Well, Brian used to say that too and look how it turned out for him. Let us tell you, Brian was not a stupid person.

He had a 4.5 GPA, 32 ACT score, was 4-handicap golfer, and was accepted to University of North Carolina at Chapel Hill, which is where he wanted to go to college. Brian always made good decisions until alcohol was involved. You see, you can't make good decisions when you drink alcohol. No matter how much you think you can, you can't. Brian proved that.

He is now frozen in time at age 18 with no chance to move forward or make a difference.

As for you, you are very much alive and able to make your destiny what you want. This is a very defining time in your life because at this moment you are able to choose the path in life you wish to follow. At this moment, you have the chance to change the way others think by taking a stand against drinking, especially drinking and driving. You are able to define who you are and to make a difference now. Be a leader and make it cool not to drink.

It is a privilege to be alive and to be able to make a difference in the lives of others. Brian lost that chance with a bad decision, but we're sure he wouldn't make that same mistake twice. But for Brian, there is no second chance. No chance to redo things. As for you, you still have the chance to make a difference in your life and in the lives of others.

If we could ask you to remember just one thing from this letter, it would be to have fun without drinking. Be a leader and make it cool not to drink. You can do it. We know you can.

And lastly, but most importantly, don't drink and drive or ride with someone who has been drinking. If you could feel for only a brief moment the extreme anguish and pain that we as a family feel over Brian's death every moment of every day, then you would understand what drinking can cost you and your family. Please think about it.

Think about what Brian lost, all his hopes, dreams and ultimately his life, as a result of alcohol. Please stay safe and don't put your family through what we are going through.

The Hoeflinger Family

Brian would have graduated June 6 from Ottawa Hills High School. He had attended St. John's Jesuit High School for three years; their commencement is May 23. His elementary school friends from St. Joe's Sylvania are graduating from schools all over the area. Many of his friends from Toledo Junior Golf are also graduating.

You may be one of those friends, or know someone who knew Brian. As you are going through the fun and excitement of these final days, preparing for prom, graduation ceremonies, and the parties of all your friends, think of us. There are no prom pictures to take, no corsage to match to a date's dress. During graduation, we will be sitting in the audience, not the proud parents of a wonderful son accepting his diploma with his classmates, but the parents choking back tears of grief and regret that he is not there.

We are the grieving father who will never golf again with his beloved son or be able to watch golf on TV without a hole in his heart. We are the mother suffering over the loss of the opportunity to excitedly plan the graduation party, shop for bedding for the dorm room and cry when she says goodbye in the fall. We are the siblings mourning the death of the brother they all looked up to. For us, this is the harsh reality of teenage drinking.

Letter #2

Hoeflingers: A Second Letter to All Teenagers

We want to start this letter by telling you a little bit about our son Brian. As you may know, he died about four months ago in an alcohol-related car accident. He had been drinking vodka at a party with friends the night he died and ended up driving intoxicated. What you don't know about Brian is that he was not known for drinking. Drinking was the least of what Brian stood for.

After much inquiry following his death, it turns out he started drinking alcohol this past summer just before starting his senior year of high school at a new school. Since his death, we have spent many sleepless nights wondering why he felt the need to start drinking. Brian was a very confident person and didn't seem to give in to peer pressure. If he had something to say, he would say it and not worry about what others thought.

But something changed his mind about drinking. Was it that everybody was doing it or that he thought it would be a new fun experience? Was it trying to fit in at a new school or trying to look cool? Or was it a little bit of all of these things?

As a teenager, you would probably know better than us because you may be going through the same thing right now or may have gone through this in the past. We also want you to know that Brian was against drinking and driving. Given that Brian was 18 years old, we had no reason not to believe that he was starting to experiment with alcohol. We knew that he was most likely starting to drink occasionally, thus we would talk to him about drinking, especially the dangers of drinking and driving. He would often tell us that he would never drink and drive and thought it was irresponsible and selfish. He would say, "I'm not that stupid, Mom." But when alcohol is involved, you can't make good decisions. Your good intentions turn into bad decisions.

Brian made a bad decision that night and it cost him his life.

We think Brian thought drinking was innocent enough when done in a controlled environment with friends. What could happen? Well, we all know how that story turned out. Dying in a horrific car accident alone was not what Brian was expecting that Friday night. He was just having fun with friends. No harm in a little fun, right? He even wore his seat belt when he left the party that night. But what he underestimated were the effects of alcohol.

You cannot make good decisions when you drink alcohol!

That one statement should mean everything to you and be seared into your mind forever. At your age, you don't think anything bad can happen to you. It can. You feel invincible. You're not. We're being brutally honest with you about our son Brian because we don't want you to make the same mistake that he did. Good kids will continue to be injured and die as long as teenage drinking continues.

The No. 1 Cause of Death

Alcohol-related accidents are the No. 1 cause of death in teenagers. An average of 80,000 deaths per year are related to drinking. Teenagers who binge drink are 14 times more likely to drink and drive than those who do not. Statistics show that on average one person will die every 53 minutes and one person will be injured every 90 seconds as a result of drinking and driving. Nothing can ever change these statistics unless someone tries to change the way we view alcohol and teenage drinking. Nearly 80 percent of all students have tried alcohol by the end of high school and 62 percent of all seniors have been drunk. Twenty five percent of ninth graders and 50 percent of tenth graders have been drunk. One in five teens binge drink. Only one in 100 parents believes his or her teen binge drinks.

Setting the Example

Drinking has become a way of life for many in high school. Did you know that 90 percent of alcoholics first start drinking as teenagers? All of you have the power to say no to alcohol. But you have to want to. Let us tell you that each of you has it within yourself to be a leader and say no to alcohol. If enough of you make a stand against teenage drinking and say no, then others will follow. When enough people follow your lead, then the minority will eventually become the majority. Only then will change happen.

So make it your goal to stop drinking and set the example for others to stop. Especially set an example for your junior classmates as they are so influenced by your actions and what you do. If you stop drinking, then they most likely will, too. Trust us, it will happen. But someone has to start this trend. Be a leader and let it be you. Take a pledge against drinking alcohol to show others that change can happen. Help your younger classmates not to start drinking by setting a good example for them.

Parents can have an impact but it is limited.

The Risks of Drinking

As Brian's parents, we talked on many occasions with him about the risks of drinking. With a neurosurgeon for a father and a forensic pathologist for a mother, he had heard many graphic horror stories of people who have been seriously injured or died as a result of alcohol. And despite this, it happened to him, which leads us to believe that children will only listen so much to their parents. You have to change from within yourselves as a group. You have the power to influence each other much more regarding social matters than a parent ever can. If the people who drink in high school would say that it is no longer cool to drink, then drinking would quickly taper down and eventually stop. But you need to take a stand against drinking and set an example for the younger students. By making this change, you are not only helping yourself but you are helping to protect your younger brother or sister from the pressure they will eventually face to drink.

And for those of you who don't drink, we applaud your courage to stand up for what you believe in. You are making a difference for the better every day. To this end, we have created a memorial website for our son Brian. The website has many articles, pictures, quotes and videos which exemplify Brian's personality as well as his many achievements. There is a donation page with a direct link to Brian's memorial fund which will ultimately be used to benefit charitable organizations or even to assist with alcohol abuse prevention in the future.

Lastly, we have posted a pledge sheet against drinking for teens to sign. If you want to help make a difference and start saving lives, then show everyone that you are not afraid to change the way things are by taking the pledge against teenage drinking. Remember, change can only happen if you take the charge to make it happen.

We want to leave you with a few quotes my son Brian wrote. The first quote was to a family who had lost their son in a tragic car accident approximately one year ago. He wrote,

> *Tragedy hits at the most random times but mainly to just remind us of all the wonderful things we have in this life. Sometimes it happens to good people, but God chooses them for a reason.*

Maybe Brian's reason will be to stop teenage drinking.

He also wrote,

> *Even the smallest of accomplishments is greatly appreciated in the eyes of a positive person because it's another step in the right direction.*

You may not think that you can make a difference by yourself, but even the smallest accomplishment of one can lead to positive change.

Lastly and most importantly, he wrote,

> *The No. 1 concern should be doing what makes you happy.*

We think in part, Brian was trying to say to be your own person and not what you think other people want you to be. Please don't drink just to fit in. "Just be you!" Sign our pledge against teenage drinking, which can be found on **www.brianmatters.com.**

Thanks for reading this and be the one to make a difference!

Letter #3

Hoeflinger: What Parents (and Everyone) Should Know about Teenage Drinking

Our son Brian N. Hoeflinger died in a tragic car accident on February 2, at the young age of 18. He was a senior in high school, an accomplished golfer, carried a 4.5 GPA and had his whole life ahead of him.

On the night he died, he was at an unsupervised party with friends drinking vodka and drove intoxicated. He struck a tree and was killed instantly. No one else was in the car.

I wrote this letter on May 2, three months after his death, on a beautiful spring day, a time of new life with trees blossoming and grasses turning green. I watched my children in the yard. Kevin was cleaning an old rowboat with the power washer. Julie was playing Spikeball with a half dozen friends.

As I watched the kids in the yard playing and having fun, I could feel Brian's absence. I could sense life all around me, but not his. I still get the feeling that Brian should be here with us, that his death must be a mistake or a dream. But no matter how hard I wish it, I know Brian is gone from this world and from our physical lives forever. I sat in his room yesterday and cried looking at pictures when he was a little boy. Where does that innocence go? Why as we get older do we lose the ability to have fun as we did as children?

I picked up Julie, my 14-year-old daughter, from a friend's house the other night. She and about 10 other girls and boys were singing together around a kitchen island after making chocolate chip cookies together. They were all standing there together having so much fun singing, laughing, and smiling. But soon that innocence will fade, and she and her friends will be tempted to drink alcohol. Why does drinking seem to be substituted for simple pleasures we enjoyed as children? As I watched the fun they were having together, it made me think of Brian and his friends when they were little and how much innocent fun they had together.

Why Does It Change?

I think the answer is in the way our society views alcohol. It almost seems like an acceptable rite of passage as we become young adults to drink alcohol. Many parents expect a certain degree of "innocent and harmless" drinking to occur. We did it as teenagers, so why shouldn't they? What can happen after having only a drink or two, right? But what about binge drinking, which is what most teenagers are doing? Is that OK? Was Brian's life worth the little bit of "harmless" fun he was having with his friends that night? Brian was growing up, but still somewhat a child inside. He was not a seasoned drinker and did not yet know the full dangers of alcohol and binge drinking. He did what statistics suggest many in our society do, which is to start drinking alcohol in high school. Remember, statistics show that nearly 75 to 80 percent of all students have drunk alcohol by the end of high school and 62 percent of all seniors have been drunk.

Most parents would deny that they condone their kids' drinking, but how many of them really ever try to stop it from happening? Statistics show that one in five teens binge drink. One in one hundred parents believes his or her teen binge drinks. Would their kids live without drinking? Yes! But there would be social consequences for their children. They may become less popular and may not be invited to social events involving the "in crowd" and drinking. I think for this reason many parents choose to ignore and thus indirectly condone this behavior. We all want our children to be popular and have friends. We hurt inside when our children are hurting. Thus many parents tolerate the fact that their children drink so their kids can be popular and accepted by the "in crowd." Many parents host parties and knowingly or "unknowingly" allow the kids to drink alcohol, seeing no potential harm in it.

Saying No

I'm sure there are many parents who are against drinking and have actively discouraged their children from drinking. These parents are to be commended for their efforts. But children will only listen to their parents so much. I truly think the kids have to change things from within themselves as a group. If the upper classmates in school who drink would take a leadership role and make it cool not to drink, then drinking among the younger classmates would soon stop.

But this only would work if the older kids make a stand, set an example and stop drinking.

Parents should discuss this aspect of drinking with our older kids and make them realize that they are influencing the younger kids to drink. We need to encourage our children to be leaders and set a good example for others to stop drinking. I know of a ninth grader who was asked to drink vodka by two tenth graders who got the vodka from a senior party. It is hard to say no to an upper classmate who is offering you a drink of alcohol. What if you said no? Then the rumors would start at school that you were afraid to try the vodka. It is so much easier to drink the vodka, get the recognition and ultimately the positive reinforcement of looking cool. If drinking alcohol was not cool, this scenario would play out much differently. In the case of this ninth grader, he drank the vodka, got drunk and was caught by his parents.

This is where I think parents can and should get involved and talk to their children. Talk to them about peer pressure and how to handle it. Arm your children with legitimate excuses when they are asked to drink.

"My parents smell my breath and make me take a Breathalyzer test when I get home" would be a great way to get out of drinking. "A close friend of mine died from drinking, and I don't drink because of it" would work as well. "I have a curfew of 11 p.m. and my parents wait up for me" would also work. Or just stand your ground and say, "I'm having a good time without getting drunk!"

Teach your kids legitimate ways to say no to alcohol in front of their friends. But most importantly, set limits and boundaries for them and let your children know that you do not approve of them drinking alcohol before the age of 21! I expect that many parents reading this letter may think that I am meddling in your personal family affairs. Just because my son died doesn't give me the right to try and change the way others think. I may have felt that same way before Brian died three months ago.

Going through the death of a child changes your perspective on life. I realize that it can happen to anyone and could easily happen to one of our remaining three children, Kevin, Julie or Christie. For that reason, my wife and I are going to change things if we can, if for no other reason than to protect our remaining three children from the harm of alcohol and binge drinking. I know some people will be on board with this philosophy and others will not, unless it unfortunately happens to them. Then it will become all too real for you, but only after it is too late to change things. I've been through it, and I only wish someone would have talked to me and tried to open my eyes to this underground network of teenage drinking before it was too late.

Gone Forever

Take a moment and really try to imagine for one instant that one of your children was never to return home and would be gone from your life forever. No chance to say goodbye or ever speak to or see them again. Force yourself to imagine. If you really try to put yourself in that position for just a moment and try to feel what it would be like if your child were dead, that horrible feeling of reality without your son or daughter in your future, that feeling alone would be enough for you to want to stop teenage drinking.

There is no happy medium. Just drinking a little doesn't work, because once you drink a little then you want to drink more. It's human nature. Once you drink more, then you start to make bad decisions. With bad decisions come bad outcomes, especially in your teenage years. Young adults and teenage brains are not fully developed until well into their mid-20s. The frontal lobes of the brain which control impulsivity, reason and logic are not fully developed. Thus at their young age, teenagers are much less likely to make good decisions, especially when they are under the influence of alcohol and drugs. Statistics show that injury and death from alcohol is markedly reduced after the age of 21 compared with those of a younger age.

Happening Right Now

We only write this letter and share our opinions and thoughts because of our personal experience with alcohol and the death of our son. But I want you to know that it is happening right now under our noses, and if we as a society continue to ignore this rising problem of teenage drinking, good children will continue to be injured and die needlessly. Somehow the innocence of childhood is being lost to alcohol far too soon. There is a way to stop it, but parents have to first acknowledge that it is happening. We have to stop ignoring the problem as if it doesn't exist. Only then can we start to properly address the issue and find solutions.

Which brings me back full circle to the question of where does the innocence of childhood go? Why do the majority of teenagers in this country drink alcohol? The answer may be that our society leads children to believe that it is OK to drink if it is kept secret, out of plain sight so you don't get caught. The liquor stores even sell to minors.

My son walked into a state liquor store with two other boys under the legal age and bought a 1.75-liter bottle of vodka without being carded the night he died. Some adults buy it for minors outside the liquor stores. The kids are smart and get it from their parents' houses or other adults' houses. Some parents host parties for minors and knowingly supply the alcohol to them. The older kids supply it to the younger kids. The point is that the alcohol is readily available and society sends the message that it is OK to drink if its kept secret and out of plain sight. The question is, how are we as a society going to stop underage drinking, and does anyone really care to? Change takes leadership and involvement. Standing by and doing nothing does just that: nothing. We as a society have to reinforce to our children that drinking alcohol is illegal before the age of 21 and will not be tolerated both at the community level as well as at the household level. This is not a punishment we are implementing but a plan to protect our kids and save them from unexpected injury, trauma, rape and the worst-case scenario: death.

Zero Tolerance

Stiffer penalties need to be in place for parents who host drinking parties for their children and their friends. There has to be zero tolerance! We as parents cannot continue to protect our kids when they break the law. I wish someone would have caught my son or arrested him before he drove under the influence of alcohol the night he died. Yes, he would have gotten in trouble and his image would have been tarnished, but he would still be alive and would have learned a valuable lesson for the future. You no longer have the chance to learn from your mistakes when you are dead. That sounds harsh, but that's the harsh reality of teenage drinking.

Kids have to understand that underage drinking will no longer be ignored and there will be consequences for their actions. Without this type of mentality, teens will continue to drink and good kids will continue to die as a result of alcohol and underage drinking. My son Brian was a good kid but he made a mistake. As parents, we need to talk to our kids and find out if they are drinking and why. We all worry about our children's safety and unfortunately play the odds that nothing will happen to them. But for some, the odds will turn against you and you never know who will be next. Instead of leaving your children's safety up to luck, talk to them, educate them and actively warn them against the risk of drinking alcohol at their young age. Let them clearly know that you do not approve of drinking and that there will be stiff consequences if they are caught. They certainly will live without drinking alcohol. From personal experience, I cannot say the opposite is true.

Please think strongly about what I have written, if only for your children's sake. Losing our son Brian has been the single worst experience in our lives and there are no words to express the pain, sorrow and emptiness we feel each and every day since his death. Don't let this happen to you. Remember, death and injuries from alcohol are preventable if we stop teenage drinking.

The letters which you have just read were meant to serve as food for thought and, we hope, to serve as a catalyst for change. I do not pretend to know how to stop teenage drinking. The solution will take time and effort by many. But I do hope that these letters will start a line of communication and discussion between parents and their children, as well as among the kids themselves, to recognize the real harm that comes with drinking alcohol and to hopefully prevent unnecessary injury or death in the future. If everyone who takes a drink in the future could just think of Brian prior to that first sip and remember what drinking cost him and his family, I think many of you would reconsider and decide not to drink. You can have fun without drinking—just give it a chance. Remember, you can't make good decisions once you start to drink alcohol. Brian proved that point. Please learn to have fun without drinking. We know you can!

Appendix 2

Quotes by Brian

Negativity is like a lock on the world; being positive unlocks this door to a world of infinite possibilities and opportunities.

Sometimes I wish there was no tomorrow. Think how much fun we could have today.

Even the smallest of accomplishments is greatly appreciated in the eyes of a positive person because it's another step in the right direction.

Just be you!

Tragedy hits at the most random times, but mainly to just remind us of all the wonderful things we have in this life. Sometimes it happens to good people, but God chooses them for a reason.

Life. One word that means everything to humans. Life is precious, and it is easy to forget that sometimes.

I promise to never judge a person based upon their appearance. I promise to give every individual I meet an equal chance to become my friend. And I promise to never hate a soul.

As I breathe, there is hope.

I control my own destiny and told myself I was going to create a new positive reality.

I realized that people grow the most when they are out of their comfort zones, and I took it as a challenge to grow.

Those who think positively thirst for opportunity because through opportunity one can move forward.

By thinking negatively, one will never reach his full potential because he is not allowing himself to fully harness the power of his own mind.

Essentially, a person's mindset determines how much they will enjoy the beauty of life.

Failure, to one who thinks positively, will be viewed as a stepping-stone on the path of life.

She's the right girl when every kiss feels as good as the first one.

A girl with good looks is sexy. But a girl with a good personality is beautiful.

Not supporting gay marriage is like not supporting the freedom of choice.

Number one concern should be doing what makes you happy.

There's sports. Then there's Spikeball.

It's not over till you give up, and even then it's not over because you've still got so many people who love and care about you.

Just remember when times are at their worst, things can only get better.

Gotta keep that positive outlook on everything.

Thankful for my family, friends, and the life I'm living! So many great people in my life.

Brian's Acceptance Letter to the
University of North Carolina at Chapel Hill

THE UNIVERSITY
of NORTH CAROLINA
at CHAPEL HILL

OFFICE OF UNDERGRADUATE ADMISSIONS

JACKSON HALL
CAMPUS BOX 2200
CHAPEL HILL, NC 27599-2200

T 919.966.3621
F 919.962.3045
www.admissions.unc.ed

February 4, 2013

Brian Hoeflinger
2524 Inlands Court
Ottawa Hills, OH 43615

Dear Brian:

It gives me great pleasure to offer you admission to the University of North Carolina at Chapel Hill. Over the last several months, as we have come to know you by reading and rereading your application, we have been impressed by all that you have accomplished. Even among the many strong students applying for admission this year, your academic and personal achievements have set you apart. We believe that you have an exciting future ahead of you, and we hope that Carolina will be the next step in your journey.

Because we have high hopes for you, I want to encourage you to continue preparing yourself for the challenges you will face here. The same curiosity and hard work that have brought you to this happy moment in your academic life will be crucial as you make the transition to college. Because we want you to come to Carolina ready to excel, your enrollment will depend upon your successful completion of your current academic year. We require that you continue to achieve at the level that enabled us to offer you admission; we also require that you graduate on time. Please arrange to have your final end-of-year transcript sent to us as soon as it becomes available.

As a first-year student, you will join outstanding classmates in the College of Arts and Sciences, which will be your academic home for your first two years at Carolina. Enclosed you will find a detailed description of the opportunities that await you, as well as a checklist of the steps you must take in order to complete your enrollment. Please review this information carefully, and please note that you will need to submit your response to our offer of admission no later than May 1, 2013, to guarantee your place in the class.

Again, congratulations on your admission to the University of North Carolina at Chapel Hill. I am delighted to be the first to welcome you to Carolina, and I wish you every success in the months ahead.

Sincerely,

Stephen Farmer
Vice Provost for Enrollment and Undergraduate Admissions

Author Note

The tragic death of my son has been one of the worst singular events that any parent could experience and has changed each member of my family forever. Yet through this tragedy, my wife and I have brought hope for others. As a result of Brian's death, the Brian Matters organization has arisen. This organization and our efforts have triggered a new awareness of teenage drinking. Through letters we have written and placed on numerous media outlets, parents across the country have begun to open a new line of communication with their children. My wife and I have talked to thousands of teenagers and adults in our local area regarding the topic of teenage drinking. We graphically show the tragic outcome which can occur from even one night of drinking.

In addition, we started a fund in Brian's honor which has raised $120,000 thus far to be used for charitable purposes. An organization for underprivileged children called Kids Unlimited has been the first beneficiary of Brian's fund.

Lastly, my wife and I are now speaking to Ohio State representatives to try to change legislation regarding teenage drinking, social host law, and the illegal selling of alcohol to minors. While nothing can ever change our son's death, all of our efforts will benefit others.

We are intent on turning tragedy into hope.

About the Author

Dr. Brian Hoeflinger, MD, a neurosurgeon, and Cindy Hoeflinger, MD, PhD, a retired forensic pathologist, live in Toledo, OH. They have four children, Brian, now frozen in time at age 18, Kevin 16, Julie 15, and Christie 12.